THE RI [
WAR
1939-1940

A STUDY IN LEADERSHIP, TRAINING, AND ESPRIT-DE-CORPS

by
Lieutenant Colonel Jouni Keravuori

US ARMY WAR COLLEGE
CARLISLE BARRACKS, PENNSYLVANIA 17013

15 May 1985

Table of Contents

PREFACE

This study of training and leadership in the Finnish army in preparation for war was inspired by the current holder of the General Ridgway Chair of Leadership, Colonel "Duke" Watson. In the "'Year of Leadership," it is indeed reassuring to have a mentor the caliber of Colonel D. C. Watson. This study evolved into a double edged project in order to capture both the written and oral history. In the chapters that follow, you will learn about the war itself and some lessons learned. The oral history aspect gives a live retrospective commentary, critique, and analysis of the Winter War, the training for it, and the leadership of the Finnish army by the commanders who fought the war. The tapes and translations will be given to the Military History Institute. I was pleasantly surprised by the enthusiasm with which I was received in Finland while I was conducting my research and interviews. I am also grateful to the US Army War College for supporting the research project. The USAWC Foundation made possible the presentation of War College mementos to each officer I interviewed in Finland.

The views expressed in this paper are those of the author and do not necessarily reflect the views of the Department of Defense or any of it agencies.

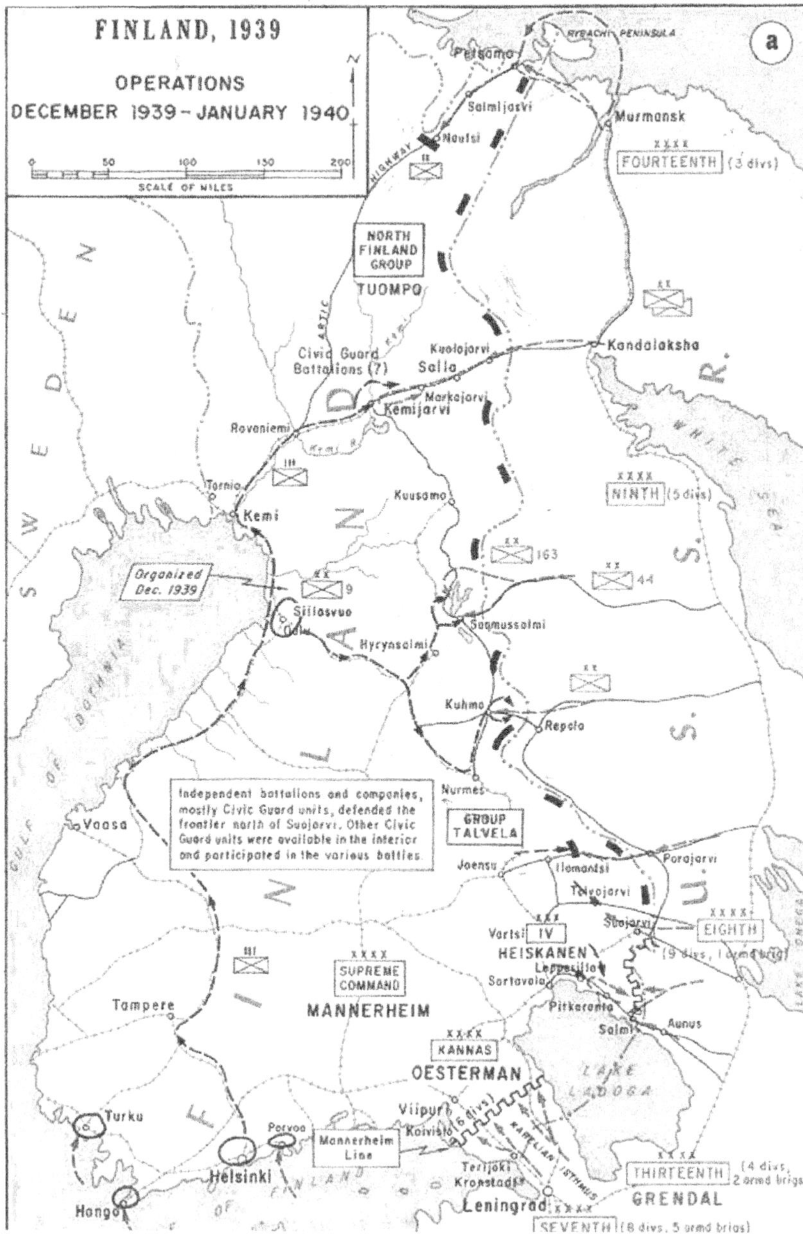

Map from U.S. Military Academy

CHAPTER I - Finland

Finland is, after Iceland, the most northerly country in the world. About one third of her total length lies north of the Arctic Circle. Geographical position: between 59°30' 10" and 70°05' 03" latitude (north); 19°07' 03" and 31°35' 20" longitude (east).

Total area: 130,128 square miles (337,032 square kilometers)

Maximum length: 724 miles (1,160 kilometers)

Maximum width: 337 miles (540 kilometers)

Coast line: 688 miles (1,100 kilometers)

Frontier: total 1,606 miles (2,571 kilometers) minus coast line

With Sweden: 336 miles (586 kilometers)

With Norway: 447 miles (716 kilometers)

With USSR: 793 miles (1,270 kilometers)

Population: about 4,500,000

Density: about 39 per square mile (15 per square kilometer)

Topography: The soil consists mainly of moraine deposits. Most of the country is low lying, rising gradually from south-southwest to north-northeast up to the fell districts of Lapland. The landscape, however, is not of the flat lowland type. It is extremely broken, with rocky hills, ridges, valleys and hollows, which usually contain lakes. The highest elevation on the "arm" at the Norwegian border is 1,328 meters.

Seas and inland waters: Finland is bounded by the Gulf of Finland and the Gulf of Bothnia. There are about 30,000 islands off the Finnish coast, mainly in the south and southwest. The 60,000 lakes comprise 9 percent of the total area. In the great lake districts of the interior, waters cover 20-50 percent of the surface.

Climate: Due to the Gulf Steam and general air currents, average temperatures are considerably higher than in other countries at the same latitude. Finland is in the snow and forest zone, characterized by warm summers and cold winters. At midsummer, there are 19 hours of daylight in South Finland. In the north, starting slightly below the Arctic Circle, there is constant daylight, which, at the 70th parallel, lasts for 73 days.

At the same latitude, there are 51 days of uninterrupted winter night during the Christmas season.

Temperatures:

July (mean): 55-62°F (13-17°C); maximum: 86°F (30°C)

February (mean): 26-7°F (-3°to -14°C); minimum: below -22° (-30°C)

January-February 1940 in the Karelian Isthmus: temperature dropped at night to -55*C.

Annual precipitation (rain and snow): Southwest Finland - 27" (700 milimeters); northwest Lapland - 24-26" (600-900 milimeters).

Distribution of land area: Arable land, 13 percent; waste land, 16 percent; forest land, 71 percent (forest land: Birch, 19 percent; Spruce, 28 percent; Pine, 53 percent).

Finland is situated almost entirely in the northern zone of coniferous forests. The oak zone in the southwest and along the south coast, however, is almost Central European in type. In Lapland, proceeding north, spruce is the first tree to disappear, followed by pine. The timber line is generally formed by dwarf birch.

Finnish language: Finnish is not an Indo-European language, but together with Estonian, Hungarian and the languages of certain national minorities in Central and North Russia, forms part of the Finno-Ugrian family of languages totaling some 21-22 million people. Finnish, like Italian, is an euphonious language, with a wealth of vowels. Short or long vowels can occur in any syllable: vaja, for instance, is "shed," but vaaja means "wedge" and vajaa, "scant." Diphthongs are common and the language has relatively few consonants. Orthography is simple,

Finnish is entirely phonetic. Pronunciation is easy, the main stress falls always on the first syllable. Finnish is a highly inflected language, without articles or genders.
Other languages: In Finland, there is a Swedish-speaking minority. Part of it descended from the Swedes who immigrated between the 9th and 13th centuries, part, of Finnish ancestry, adopted Swedish when it was the language of the educated. People who speak Swedish as mother tongue make about six percent of the population. Lapp, also a Finno-Ugrian language, is spoken by 3,500 persons in Finnish Lapland.
According to the constitution, Finnish and Swedish are the official languages of the Republic of Finland.

History of Finland:

1155: The first Swedish crusade to Finland; Finland becomes part of the Kingdom of Sweden.
1809: Sweden surrenders Finland to Russia. Czar makes Finland an autonomous Grand Duchy.
1917: Finnish declaration of independence on 6 December; first recognized by Russia, France, Germany and Sweden.
1919: Present constitution adopted; Finland becomes a Republic.
The growing forces of Pan-Slavism and Nationalism in Russia swelled at the end of the century with serious impact on Finland. Various attempts were made to Russify Finland and the autonomous status of the country was violated. This provoked an attitude of passive resistance in Finland and a growing desire for complete independence. On 6 December 1917, after the October Revolution of the Bolsheviks, Finland declared herself independent, but the effective beginning of the political activity had to be postponed because of the outbreak of the War of Independence on 28 January 1918. This was at first a struggle to disarm and intern the Russian forces

(about 40,000) in Finland; then it developed into a civil war between the Russian supported Reds and the patriotic Whites. Russian forces from within and without (from Leningrad and the Russian Baltic Navy) participated to the very end of the war and provided the Reds with leadership, weaponry and munitions. During the last phase of the struggle, a German division of two regiments made landings at Helsinki and Lovisa, thus hastening the final outcome, the victory of General Mannerheim's White forces. Relations between Finland and Russia remained cool, even hostile, in the 1919-1921 period when Finnish volunteers participated in campaigns with the East-Karelians for the purpose of securing the Karelians' independence from Russia.

Peace was concluded in Tartu, Estonia, in 1920.

The State of Finland: Finland is a sovereign Republic. The constitution was adopted in 1919. The legislative power is exercised by Parliament in conjunction with the President. The supreme executive power is vested in the President, who shall make his decisions in the Councils of State (Cabinet) upon the report of the Minister to whose competency the question involved belongs. The judicial power is vested in independent Courts of Justice.

The President of Finland is elected for a term of six years by an Electoral College of 300. He can veto a bill passed by Parliament, but a bill thus suspended will become a law if Parliament, after a general election, passes it without amendment. The President can issue decrees and ordinances containing no provisions implying a modification of a law. He is the Commander-in-Chief of Armed Forces, although he may delegate his authority in time of war. The President is responsible for Finland's relations with foreign powers, although decisions of war and peace and more important treaties concluded with foreign powers must be approved by Parliament.

Parliament has consisted of a single chamber since 1906. The members, 200 in number, are elected by proportional representation. Suffrage is equal and universal, all citizens over the age of 18 having the right to vote.
The Cabinet, presided over by the Prime Minister, is responsible for the general conduct of administrative affairs. Its members, who must enjoy the confidence of Parliament, are appointed by the President.
The rights and duties of citizens are laid down in the Constitution. The most important rights are equality before the law; security of life, liberty and property; protection of labor; freedom of worship, speech, meeting, and association. Duties include compulsory military service.

MILITARY-POLITICAL DEVELOPMENT IN EUROPE BEGINNING IN 1938

1. Austrian Anschluss in March 1938.
2. Munich Pact in September 1938.
3. Czechoslovakian crisis in September 1938.
4. Southern part of Slovakia ceded to Hungary in November 1938.
5. Slovakia declares independence in March 1939.
6. Germany occupies Western Czechoslovakia in March 1939.
7. Germany occupies Southern Lithuania (Memel) in March 1939.
8. Britain and France initiate negotiations with USSR to contain Germany in March 1939.
9. Italy occupies Albania in April 1939.
10. USSR proposes to secure agreement with Britain and France which would recognize the Baltic States and Finland as being within the Soviet sphere of influence.
11. Finland makes strong protests in London and Paris.
12. The Allies declare that any proposal which include Finland would be unacceptable.

13. Anglo-Franco-Russo discussions fail.
14. USSR initiates trade negotiations with Germany in April 1939.
15. Germany initiates non-aggression pact negotiations with Finland and the Scandinavian countries. Finland refused the offer as violation of neutrality and Scandinavian orientation.
16. Molotov-Ribbentrop Pact on 23 August 1939.
17. Mutual Assistance Pact between Britain and Poland in August 1939.
18. German invasion of Poland on 1 September 1939.
19. The fourth partition of Poland on 17 September 1939.
20. Estonia, Latvia and Lithuania accede to Soviet demands for military bases on 28 September, 5 October and 11 October, respectively.

SOVIET UNION INITIATES NEGOTIATIONS WITH FINLAND

1. The Second Secretary of the Soviet Legation in Helsinki, Boris Yartsev, requested an appointment with the Finnish Foreign Minister Holsti. A series of discussions followed which lasted for almost a year and brought Soviet apprehensions and intentions into the open. Secretary Yartsev proposed that:
a. Finland guarantee not to aid Germany in any war against the Soviet Union.
b. Soviet Union sign a commercial treaty with Finland.
c. Other proposals were vague, and discussions dragged on into the summer and autumn of 1938.
2. Finland proposed a draft treaty by which she would continue to adhere to her policy of neutrality and would permit no violation of her territory or its use by any great power for an attack upon the Soviet Union, and provided that Finland be granted Soviet permission to fortify the Aaland Islands as a safeguard of her neutrality.

3. A Soviet counterproposal on 18 August suggested that Finland merely enter into a written understanding that she would resist any German aggression and would call upon Russia for aid if unsuccessful. Russian "aid" in this case was not specified; but Finland was to procure arms from Russia, and to allow the construction of a Soviet airbase on Suursaari Island in the Gulf of Finland. In return, Russia was prepared to allow Finland to fortify the Aaland Island with Soviet help, supervision, and partial control, and to sign a treaty guaranteeing Finnish territorial integrity and sovereignty. In addition, Russia would enter into a trade agreement favorable to Finland.
4. In a full session of the Finnish government, it was decided to reject the Soviet proposal on the grounds that "the proposal tends to violate Finland's sovereignty and is in conflict with the policy of neutrality which Finland follows in common with the nations of Scandinavia."
5. The Soviet Union did not pursue the matter at the time.
6. The Kremlin refused to enter into a trade agreement until political and military questions were resolved.
7. In March, Moscow proposed that some of the islands in the Gulf of Finland be leased to the Soviet Union as observation posts. When Finland refused, it was suggested that the islands be ceded to the Soviet Union in exchange for territory in East Karelia. The Finnish government turned down the proposal. It felt that if Finland acceded to the Soviet demands, nothing would restrain Germany from making similar demands.
8. The political/military negotiations were broken off and the trade negotiations discontinued.
9. On 5 October, Foreign Minister Molotov requested Finnish Foreign Minister Erkko to come to Moscow to discuss "certain concrete questions of a political nature." When, by the 8th, the Finnish government had not replied, the Soviet Ambassador in Helsinki called on Erkko to impress upon him the need for haste, pointing

out that Finland was not treating the matter as the other Baltic states had.

10. Finland decided not to send Erkko, the Foreign Minister, since it was felt that Erkko's place was with the government. Instead, Finnish envoy to Stockholm, J. K. Paasikivi was selected to head the Finnish delegation to Moscow. The Finnish government instructed Paasikivi to emphasize that Finland's policy of neutrality, her small size, the Treaty of Tartu (1922), and the Nonaggression Pact with the USSR militated against her becoming a threat to the Soviet Union. Also, any territorial concessions were to be ruled out, as was the establishment of Soviet military bases on the Finnish mainland, or on the Aaland Islands, and any territorial adjustments on the Karelian Isthmus. Only under extreme pressure was Paasikivi to concede some small islands in the Gulf of Finland, but not Suursaari. Any concessions were to be reciprocal, and the compensation would have to appear reasonable to the world. Finally, no discussions of a mutual assistance treaty was permitted.

11. Stalin demanded everything Paasikivi was forbidden to discuss:

a. A mutual assistance treaty

b. The lease of naval base for stationing 5,000 troops on Hanko cape at the mouth of the Gulf of Finland.

c. The western part of the Fisherman's Peninsula on the Arctic Ocean.

d. The removal of the Finno-Soviet border on the Karelian Isthmus some twelve kilometers farther from Leningrad.

e. Some islands in the Gulf of Finland, including Suursaari.

f. Stalin suggested the demolition of fortifications on both sides of the frontier because they were "prejudicial to peaceful relations."

12. Unprepared for the magnitude of the Soviet demands, Paasikivi returned to Helsinki for new instructions. There, the Finnish government concluded that under no circumstances could Hanko be leased to the USSR; on the other hand, five small islands could be ceded for compensation, a small westward adjustment of the Karelian border could be accepted, and the 1932 Nonaggression Pact could be drafted to state that neither party would aid another state attacking one of the contracting powers. If it became necessary, Paasikivi was also authorized to cede the southern part of Suursaari and, if pressed, the whole island, to keep Hanko out of jeopardy. With regard to the Fisherman's Peninsula, there was to be no yielding.

13. Unwilling to conduct the negotiations without a member of his government present, Paasikivi was accompanied by Minister Tanner on his return to Moscow. When the new proposals were presented to Stalin on the 23rd, he declared them inadequate, insisting that the Soviet demands were minimal and could not be reduced by bargaining. After some two hours of futile discussions, the session ended, and Paasikivi and Tanner prepared to return to Helsinki; but a few hours later, Molotov's secretary appeared at the Finnish Legation to request their presence for another meeting. When they arrived at the Kremlin, Stalin began as though there had been no break in the discussions. He offered to reduce the number of troops on Hanko to 4,000, to decrease the territorial demands on the Karelian Isthmus, and to accept the Finnish proposal for the expansion of the Nonaggression Pact.

14. The first two demands remained more than the Finns were willing to concede; even 4,000 troops at Hanko laid Finland's heavily populated industrial heartland open to attack from within, and the shift in the border would still place it dangerously near Viipuri. Unable to commit their

government to these proposals, Paasikivi and Tanner returned to Helsinki for consultations. At the same time, Tanner addressed an inquiry to the Swedish government asking whether Finland could expect its support in the event of war. On 27 October, the Swedish Prime Minister Hansson replied that Sweden would continue to supply Finland with arms, munitions, equipment, food, and diplomatic support, but nothing more was to be expected for fear of German reprisals.

15. The Finns, virtually left to their own devices, moved into the final phase of the negotiations. After intensive negotiations and discussions in the cabinet, and with the party leaders in the Parliament, a firm stand was taken against Stalin's proposals. No base was to be leased at Hanko, but the border might be moved somewhat westwards on the Isthmus, the western part of the Fisherman's Peninsula could be ceded, and the small islands in the Gulf of Finland were again offered. Stalin's suggestions that the fortifications on both sides of the Karelian frontier be demolished was also refused on the grounds that Finland's fortifications were required only for defense and for the preservation of Finnish neutrality.

16. En route to Moscow, Paasikivi and Tanner received word that Molotov had announced the full details of the negotiations in his speech to the Supreme Soviet on 31 October. However, the Finns decided to continue to Moscow in the hopes that there would still be room for negotiations. Their optimism proved unfounded, for the Finnish proposals were declared inadequate almost before they were fully presented, and no further compromises were forthcoming from Stalin. Before leaving the Kremlin, Molotov remarked, "We civilians can see no further in the matter; now it is the turn of the military to have their say." On this ominous note, the Finns departed for home.

17. Throughout November, matters were relatively calm in spite of a steady stream of abuse against Finland in the Soviet press and repeated violations of Finnish airspace by Soviet aircraft. However, an optimism prevailed in the Finnish government that a bad phase had passed and affairs with Russia would improve. This feeling was strengthened by a report on the 23rd that the American Ambassador to Moscow did not believe the USSR would attack Finland.
18. In a note on 26 November, the Finnish army was accused of an artillery attack at the village of Mainila. Molotov proposed that Finnish troops be withdrawn some 25 kilometers from the frontier to "preclude all possibility of a repetition of provocative acts." From this point, relations rapidly deteriorated between the neighbors. Everyone knew that the purpose of this provocation was to scare the Finns to such an extent that they would vacate the defensive positions along the border region, and, on the other hand, to put the blame on the Finnish government for provoking an armed conflict.
19. The Finns, however, declared their willingness to negotiate a mutual withdrawal of troops from the border and also suggested a joint committee to investigate the incident. On 28 November, Molotov rejected the Finnish proposals, accusing the Finnish government of "harboring deep hostility towards the USSR." Molotov then stated that Finland no longer abided by the Nonaggression Pact and announced the Soviet Union's unilateral renunciation of the Pact.
20. Without waiting for a Finnish reply to his note, Molotov announced the Soviet Union's severance of diplomatic relations with Finland on 29 November.
21. Still bending every effort to avoid war, the Finnish government sent a conciliatory reply to the previous day's note and recommended a joint investigation with a view to a peaceful settlement of the dispute. The Finns also

agreed to withdraw all but units of the frontier guard and customs officials to such a distance from Leningrad as to no longer constitute a threat to the city. During the same day, however, a Russian force crossed the border at Petsamo and took several Finnish border guards prisoner. The full Soviet answer to the Finnish note came on the 30th in an all out attack upon Finland by land, sea, and air. That morning, Russian bombers out of their bases in Estonia, dived low over Helsinki and other cities to unload their cargoes of bombs. According to the Russian radio, the Finnish reports of these air raids were fabrications, for the Red Air Force had merely dropped bread to the starving masses of Helsinki. Thereafter, the Finns referred to Russian bombs as "Molotov's bread baskets."

THE ORDER OF THE DAY OF THE LENINGRAD MILITARY DISTRICT ON 30 NOVEMBER 1939

"Red Army Comrades, Commanders, Commissars and Political Advisers! To fulfill the desires of the Council of Ministers of the Soviet Socialist Republic and the holy will of our great State, I order the forces of the Leningrad Military District to cross the frontier, destroy the Finnish forces and, once and for all, secure the northwestern border of the Soviet Socialist Republic, and the safety of the city of Leningrad, the cradle of the proletarian revolution.

We will not enter the territory of Finland as conquerors but as friends of the Finnish people and as their liberators from the yoke of the big landlords and capitalists.

We will not oppose the Finnish people but the Cajander-Erkko clique which has oppressed the Finnish people and provoked the war against the Soviet Socialist Republic.

We honor Finland's liberty and independence which the Finnish people obtained through the October Socialist revolution and through the victory by the Soviet people.

For this independence fought together with the Finnish people the Russian bolsheviks, Messrs. Lenin and Stalin in the foreground.

The War Council has become firmly convinced that the Leningrad Military District will fulfill its duty for our fatherland with honor, totally destroy the enemy forces and thus forever prevent the warmongers' access to the Gulf of Finland and Leningrad."

Signed by

K. A. Meretskov, 2nd Class

Army Commander

The above military order unleashed the Russian forces which had been concentrated along the Finno-Russian border. Their mobilization to the full strength began in September 1939, in conjunction with the Red Army's crossing the Polish border on 17 September 1939.

CHAPTER II - The Genesis of Training the Finnish Soldier

The training of Finnish soldiers to fight Russians began hundreds of years ago. Russians often attacked Finland during the centuries the country was a Swedish territory (1100 to 1809). Finnish peasants and farmers succeeded time after time in pushing the Russians back to their country. The origins of a Finnish protective corps of volunteers has long roots.

History offers many examples of these campaigns. The battle of Joutselka, 11 March 1555, is perhaps best known in Finland. The Finnish ski patrols observed thousands of cossacks approaching, horses wading in deep snow. The fast ski patrols informed the peasants who then hastily built an obstacle on the road. Several hundred (perhaps 500-600) skiers waited in the woods. The cossacks were surprised to see an obstacle (heavy logs) on the road. Suddenly there were skiers on both sides of the column. Thousands of cossacks were killed, and the survivors returned to Russia. The same tactics were used successfully 400 years later in the Finnish-Russian war.

During the Middle Ages, Finland was a Swedish territory. Every Finnish generation fought Russians, protecting their own area and Sweden. There were 24 wars from 1515 to 1721 (148 war years, 58 years of peace). The worst time for the Finns was the so called "Great Hatred" during the rule of Peter the Great in the beginning of the 1700's. The Protective Corps was an idea strengthened in Finnish minds at that time because the Finns began to lose faith in Sweden as the defender of the Kingdom.

In 1809 Finland was ceded to the Russian Czar, Alexander I, who promised to retain Finland's constitution. Alexander II (1855-1870) was the best czar

from the Finnish viewpoint. During his time, several good measures happened:
Finland established its own senate, the cultural life blossomed, educational development advanced. There is no illiteracy in Finland because the church did not let anybody get married unless both were able to read and write.
Finland also had its own Army.
In 1894 Nicolaus II became the Russian Czar. He had many problems in his personal Life. Rasputin provided ill council. His son (Alexis) was a hemophiliac. Additionally, Nicolaus was a weak leader. In Finland this was a period of oppression. The cultural life was suppressed, Russian language was made mandatory in schools. Finland's army activities were disbanded.
The Finnish reaction reawakened the idea of the Protective Corps. Several other things took place during this period. Approximately 2,000 young men left secretly to go to Germany for military training. First, they approached Sweden but the Swedes refused to cooperate. In 1914 the Jagerbattalion was established in the eastern part of Germany. After their training period, these young men fought Russians on the Eastern Front with the Germans. They returned to Finland in February 1918, when the Independence war had already begun. They formed the major part of the leadership of the forces fighting in the Independence war.
During the Nicolas II rule, the Russification program of Finland was carried on, especially in 1904-1917. Many patriotic people joined the so called "fire departments." Men who had little experience gave the "fire departments" preliminary military training. At the same time, communism, which came from Germany, got a foothold among Finnish workers. Unfortunately, the communists found out the activities of the fire departments. They did not understand and they did not

want to support the purposes of the Protective Corps, which was to prepare for the independence campaign.

During this period many outstanding citizens worked with young people. In 1917 Lauri Pihkala,who was a well known athletic coach, wrote articles and gave speeches in many parts of the country. All sports minded people respected him and thus the Protective Corps received thousands of enthusiastic members.

The 1917 elections in Finland indicated that the leftists had lost votes. The communist leaders (Red guards) had met and considered what problems they had. They knew that the Russian troops which had remained in Finland after the Russian revolution in March 1917 would join them to fight the Protective Corps. There were approximately 30,000 Russian army troops in different towns in eastern and southern parts of Finland and approximately 20,000 Russian navy men.

The Protective Corps consisted at the same time (Fall 1917) of about 14,000 men. By January 1918, the Protective Corps organization had spread to most cities and villages throughout Finland. In December 1917 (then) Lieutenant General Mannerheim arrived from the Russian frontline to his native land. He became the Chief of the Protective Corps, and later the Marshal of Finland. In January 1918, P. E. Svinhufvud,who had been a Russian prisoner in Siberia, was now in charge of the Finland government. He gave Mannerheim the authority to lead the military activities to restore order to the country. Mannerheim's idea was that Finland must secure freedom by its own power and not rely on Germany or other foreign countries. He knew well the turmoil, inefficiency, and the state of decay of the Russian armed forces.

The communist (Red) leaders explained to their people that the Protective Corps were "butchers" whose intention

was to suppress the workers. This propaganda lived for a long time.
Finland's new government announced on 25 January 1918 that the Protective Corps were now official government troops. This action sharply divided Finland into patriotic and socialist camps, White versus Red.

White and Red Finland

On 28 January 1918, the civil war began. It was a bitter, sometimes violent, campaign which is common when citizens of the same nation are fighting each other. The war lasted three and a half months. The Russian troops had been pushed back to Russia; Red Finnish troops had been defeated, many
of them were now prisoners of war.
On 2 August 1918, the Parliament decided to accept the statute of the Protective Corps.

The Statute of the Protective Corps

The purpose of the Protective Corps is, with direction by the government, to promote the pecople's defense capability and protect lawful community activity. To do this, the Protective Corps will:
a. give military education to its members;
b. advance gymnastics, athletics (sports) and promote citizenship;
c. act, when necessary, as a support element of the regular army; and
d. assist, when requested, the police force.
Men, whose loyalty toward the lawful society can be trusted, might be accepted as members. They must be at least 17 years old. In exceptional cases, and by permission of their parents, even younger men can be accepted.
In this statute were several paragraphs which did not change during the entire life of the Protective Corps.

However, during the first year, it was realized that drafting young men into the armed forces should be done by a special draft board, not by the Protective Corps. The final decision concerning this was made in 1919.

In the following ten years the Protective Corps' activity advanced in many areas. The idea of an officers' school was developed in 1919. The school began functioning the following year, and by 1925 it was fully operational. Its location was only approximately 25 miles from Helsinki.

Perhaps the most difficult problem was the financial situation. Finland was at that time (1919-1929) a rather poor agricultural country. However, they had dreamed to be a free country, and when that dream became real, they were willing to give what they had. The Protective Corps did not have any arms, they had no uniforms, they did not have any other facilities, not even barracks in which to train the members, etc. However, private persons, city councils (even small communities), small and large factories, lumber companies, etc., began to give funds to the Protective Corps. Hundreds of communities held numerous festival and entertainment events, getting money for the Corps. It has to be emphasized that these festivals had generally very dignified and patriotic programs.

The best results concerning the contributions were naturally achieved in the southern and western parts of Finland. Many northern and eastern poor communities had to wait for years before they received enough funds for uniforms, weapons and equipment.

In 1921, General Malmberg became chief of the Protective Corps. The women's organization was also begun in 1921, with the name of Lotta-Svard.

Lotta-Svard

The name is derived from a historical poem which tells the story of a woman who helped men in combat, bringing them food, giving wounded men first-aid and guiding men ("medics") who took the wounded to the first-aid station.

Lotta-Svard's purpose was also to augment the Protective Corps and to protect religion, home and the country. This was done by:

a. acting to create the will to defend the nation;

b. assisting the Corps medical work;

c. assisting to feed the Protective Corps men;

d. assisting to get suitable clothing to the men; and

e. assisting office and communication work and helping to get funds to do its mission.

It must be emphasized that the Protective Corps members were all volunteers without pay. They joined the Corps to be able to protect their country. Only the permanent, regular officers were paid. In the beginning, many members paid for their uniforms and weapons, but later the Headquarters of the Protective Corps provided them.

Military training emphasized combat skills in both summer and winter. In southern and western Finland, the training periods were weekly, but in the northern and eastern part of the country where distances are longer (some communities are in a several hundred square miles area), the training periods were organized at convenient times for farmers, laborers, lumberjacks, students, white collar workers, etc. Then the training periods lasted at least a week, and employers gave them free time for these activities.

Firing ranges for rifle practice were gradually built in all parts of the country, and firing became an important part of the training program. All districts had hundreds of competitions during the year. Biathlon (ski firing) was added to the program already started in the 1920's. It was realized that the men who were good in the biathlon race were effective fighters in wartime; this fact became obvious during World War II.

From the very beginning, leaders understood the importance of physical training. Cross country skiing was most important in wintertime and provided also endurance for summertime activities. Hundreds of ski competitions were held by the communities (villages, towns, schools) and districts; and once a year the best people of all twenty two Protective Corps districts competed for the championships of the entire country. Fortunately skiing before World War II was the most important means of transportation in wintertime. Biathlon competitions were added to the program in 1925. When a man, carrying a rifle on his back, has skied fast four to eight miles, is perspiring and breathless, and is able to hit a small target at 200 yards, he develops self confidence. He is convinced that he can hit an enemy in combat.

Orienteering competitions were also started in 1925, and today orienteering has spread to all Scandinavian countries. It is now done in both summer and winter. Orienteering was very beneficial training. During the Finnish-Russian war, 1939-44, the Finnish ski patrols and troops were skilled in wilderness navigation, day and night, summer and winter.

Annual gymnastic festivals were held in the summertime. Over 150,000 men, women, boys and girls prepared during the winter for these events held in local gymnasiums.

The Protective Corps started youth activities, establishing boys' "detachments" in all communities before 1930. Their program was somewhat similar to the Boy Scout work. The boys also played "terrain races," learning concealment and camouflaging. They participated, by age groups, in skiing, orienteering, firing (22 rifle), and several other competitions. These young men became the Corps volunteers in subsequent years.

In 1925, all districts received so called educational advisors, whose mission was to promote Protective Corps activities and to foster strong patriotic feelings. During the following years, these advisors enjoyed success; they organized thousands of occasions where patriotic speeches were delivered. About a million people participated each year between 1925-1939. Several Protective Corps magazines were published all over the country. Most of the clergymen volunteered to serve as Protective Corps pastors.

In summary, the Protective Corps served the Finns to great advantage. It built the foundation for a strong national spirit. It provided an organization which complemented the military district and mobilization systems. It trained young men in the most essential soldiering skills. Upon entering the army, Protective Corps members were exempt from much of the preliminary training. These men were physically fit, expert marksmen, and able navigators, all vital skills used during the Winter War. More importantly, however, there was a deep national spirit reinforced by unit cohesion that became a combat multiplier.

CHAPTER III - The Winter War

Finnish Defense Forces on the Eve of the Winter War

Since Finland's independence (1917), it had been commonly accepted among all Finns but especially the military that the only potential enemy was Russia. Therefore, the nation was prepared psychologically and defensively to fight the enemy from the east. Military service had been compulsory since 1922, with provisions for one year conscription service, 18 months for those to be trained for officers and non-commissioned officers, and reserve service until age 50 for all others except officers who were obligated to serve until age 60.

Since 1934 the national defense forces were organized on a territorial basis, so that the complete units could be assembled, organized and equipped near their home areas and transferred to the front in a minimum of time, normally within a week after the first alert. However, the implementation of this system was possible only by drawing money from the allocations planned for buying materiel and equipment. An additional 10 percent cut in the defense budget in 1932-1933 further decreased the preparedness of the armed forces. Thus Finland was only beginning to develop her defense forces upward to the standards that would have met the minimum requirements when the so called "Mainila shots" were fired and the Red Army crossed the 1,500 kilometer long frontier on 30 November 1939.

On the eve of the war, the organization of the Finnish defense forces was as follows. There were about 300,000 men in age groups of 20-40 who had received military training. The equipment available, however, was only for an army of 275,000. According to Marshal Mannerheim, the Finnish army had at the beginning of the war the following amount of ammunition, fuel and lubricating oils: two months' supply of small arms ammunition, fuel and lubricating oils; one months' supply of aviation fuel; and three weeks supply of 76mm and 122mm light field artillery, 81mm mortar and 150mm and 152mm artillery rounds.

These deficiencies were partially adjusted by purchases and shipments from Sweden and other countries. Some items, however, arrived much too late, i.e., the US Navy Brewster aircraft which were shipped to Norway, assembled there and then flown to Finland. Only a few of the 40 purchased arrived at Finland before the end of the war.

Mobilization and Concentration of Forces

According to the mobilization plan, the regular army units and those reserve units which were to be mobilized from reservists living within the Karelian Isthmus and within the border regions between Lake Ladoga and the Arctic Ocean were to be used as a screening and covering force. Their mission was to delay the enemy forces' advance until the field army forces had been concentrated into their respective sectors along the selected main lines of defense. On the Karelian Isthmus front, the screening forces consisted of 14 battalions and 9 separate companies. On the frontier between Lake Ladoga and the Arctic Ocean, only one territorial battalion to be organized by the Frontier Guards and equipped with only light weapons was to perform the screening and covering mission along each road leading from the border westwards.

Some of these units were alerted already in September 1939, immediately after Germany's attack on Poland. All screening and covering forces were in their respective areas by 10 October. On the Karelian Isthmus, the 14 battalions and 9 separate companies were organized into four separate groups.

a. The Uusikirkko (U) Group was responsible for delaying the enemy's advance along the zone between the Gulf of Finland and the line from Joutselka on the border to Suulajarvi Lake Perkjarvi Lake, Muolaanjarvi Lake, Kamaranjarvi Lake. The screening and covering mission on this 40 kilometer wide and over 70 kilometer deep zone was assigned to a force consisting of two squadrons of cavalry, a light bicycle battalion, two Civil Guard battalions and two border companies. Its artillery support consisted of a battery of light 76mm guns. Its anti-tank defense was made of four 37mm guns and individual tank destroyers.

b. The Muolaa (M) group consisted of a light bicycle battalion, a Civil Guard battalion and two border companies.

c. The Lipola (L) group consisted of a light bicycle battalion, a Civil Guard battalion and two border companies.

d. The Rautu (R) group consisted of a light bicycle battalion, a Civil Guard battalion and two border companies.

e. The remaining three battalions were in reserve behind the R group which had the shallowest zone along which to delay the enemy.

In the middle of October the Finnish field army's eight divisions and their support units were at their respective sectors. They were deployed as follows:

a. The Army of the Karelian Isthmus (six divisions) was divided into two army corps, namely, the II Corps on the right and the III Corps on the left.

b. The Commander-in-Chief's reserve, the Sixth Division, in the vicinity of Viipuri, engaged in preparing field fortifications along the western end of the Viipuri-Vuoksi River line.

c. IV Corps consisted of two divisions situated along the almost 100 kilometer wide front north of Lake Ladoga with its left flank at Suojarvi Lake.
d. The 9th Division was being assembled and equipped at Oulu. At this time there were weapons and some field equipment for only one of its infantry regiments. Its artillery regiment was being organized without guns.

The Waiting Period

During the prolonged negotiations with the Russians which began on 12 October in the Kremlin, Finland was able to win the first round in the war of nerves. Her forces were in place to encounter the worst, the invasion.
The field army was able to familiarize its units with the terrain and the circumstances they would utilize during the combat situation. The main defense line, the so called Mannerheim Line, was built during the waiting period. Its tank traps and the majority of the permanent fortifications had been built during the previous summer by thousands of volunteers and civilian fortification battalions; however, some fortifications were built as early as 1920's. Without these defense works, the Isthmus Army's capability to defend the main line of resistance, the Mannerheim Line, would have been greatly reduced and, perhaps, the final results of the war would have been much more disastrous for the Finnish nation.

The General Trace of the Mannerheim Line

The Mannerheim Line, which was planned as early as 1919, ran in general from Kyronniemi Cape on the Gulf of Finland in a northerly direction to Kuolemanjarvi Lake, then to Hatjalahti' Lake and further north up to the bend of the Summajoki River; from there it turned toward the east and was anchored on with the following key terrain features: the Summajarvi Lake, the Munasuo Swamp, Muolaanjarvi Lake, Yskjarvi Lake, the Church

Village of Muolaa on Kirkkojarvi Lake, PunnusJarvi Lake, Oravaniemi Cape on Vuoksi River and further along Vuoksi to Taipale River which runs into Lake Ladoga.

The Eastern Front

The Janisjoki River Line - Some permanent fortifications had been built in early 1920's along the line between Lake Ladoga and Janisjarvi Lake, but these bunkers proved to be more like "mouse traps" than secured firing positions. New fortifications were built during the summer of 1939 by volunteers and by civilian work companies on certain key locations along the Janisjoki River line and also along the line Kitila, Syskyjarvi Lake, Varpajarvi Lake, and even further along the northeastern coast of Lake Ladoga and Uuksu ans Salmi. As on the Mannerheim Line, these fortifications consisted primarily of tank traps made of boulders erected in four rows in front of the planned line of strong points.

Additional field fortifications were built along the Sortavala, Suo, Jarvi Lake railroad, primarily on narrows between the numerous lakes and alongside roads leading to the national border.

There were no fortifications of any kind along the long eastern front north of Ilomantsi.

Concentration of Russian Forces Against Finland in November 1939, and Their Assigned Strategic Objectives

On the Karelian Isthmus was the Soviet 7th Army. The objective of the 7th Army's left (western) wing was to occupy the city of Viipuri and then advance into the heartland of Finland, while its right wing crossed the Vuoksi River on the eastern part of the Isthmus and took the Sortavala-Imatra railroad, thus separating the Finnish forces by cutting their lines of communications.

On the Ladogan Karelian front between Lake Ladoga and Ilomantsi was the Soviet 8th Army. The objective of the 8th Army was to advance westward and around Lake Ladoga, and to join the eastern wing of the 7th Army, thus denying the Finnish forces the opportunity to establish any organized defense systems west of the chain of Saimaa lakes.

Further north of Ilomantsi was the Soviet 9th Army. The objective of the 9th Army was to cut Finland at her waist by a drive to the northern end of the Gulf of Bothnia, thus cutting communications with Sweden by land.

In the Arctic was the Soviet 14th Army. The 14th Army's objective was the port of Petsamo (Pechenga) and a southward advance from there to Kemijarvi-Rovaniemi as its first objective, and then the final advance to the Swedish border.

The War Begins

At twenty minutes past nine in the morning of 30 November 1939, an aircraft marked with red stars dropped propaganda leaflets over Helsinki. Ten minutes later, a group of bombers delivered more lethal messages to Viipuri in the first of many devastating raids on Finland's second largest city. Earlier that morning, the Red Army had struck with artillery, tanks, infantry and aircraft at numerous points along the 1,500 kilometer Soviet-Finnish border from Petsamo on the Arctic Ocean to the Terijoki region on the Gulf of Finland. Surprised by overwhelming forces, the Finnish guards at the observation posts were quickly killed, captured or dispersed.

On that morning the President of Finland appointed Field Marshal Viscount Mannerheim Commander-in-Chief, and a new Cabinet under the President of the Bank of Finland, Mr. Risto Ryti, which was to renew the talks with the Soviet government immediately. On the second day of the war, Stalin in turn recognized as the legal Finnish government a "Democratic People's Republic of Finland," which was composed of communist refugees which had fled from Finland to the Soviet Union in 1918, immediately after the Finnish War of Independence.

At the same time, a treaty of friendship, assistance and cooperation was concluded with this government. Referring to this treaty, the Soviet Union informed the Council of the League of Nations that it was not at war with Finland and turned down the mediation offers of the United States and Sweden. The extent of the Soviet attack as well as the forming of the puppet regime made the Finnish people realize that the whole future of the nation was at stake; by the same token, it also raised the Finn's will to fight to the utmost.

The main axis of the Soviet attack was on the Karelian Isthmus; however, the most dangerous situation developed at several locations along the long, weakly guarded eastern border.

The First Week of the War

Although the invasion was not a complete surprise, the scope and intensity of the initial offensives came as a shock to the Finnish General Staff. Four Soviet armies hurled 16 of their 25 divisions immediately available, supported by 1,700 tanks, strong artillery and aircraft against the very weak Finnish covering forces. Even more disturbing was the fact that over half of the Soviet infantry divisions, with almost one half of their tanks, were advancing virtually unopposed along wilderness roads from Lake Ladoga to the Arctic Ocean. The Finnish general staff had grossly underestimated the strength which the Russians could deploy along the few secondary roads leading from the Murmansk railroad to the Finnish border. As a consequence, there were only nine weak screening units of approximately battalion strength along the over 1,000 kilometer long frontier where the Soviet forces moved forward along nearly every frontier road in division strength. This unexpected situation exceeded the Finnish general staff's worst expectations.

The Russian columns advanced rapidly, pursuing the hopelessly outnumbered screening forces. As anti-tank weapons were totally lacking, the first sight of Soviet tanks created panic among many troops.

When Soviet forces attacked Petsamo by land, sea and air, the Finnish army could only defend it with the 10th Independent Company and one battery of four antique field guns, model 1887, which had been used there primarily for ceremonial purposes. The Soviet 14th Army rapidly achieved its first objective of securing the port of Petsamo and holding it to prevent any third parties from intervening there.

The next objective south of Petsamo was the capital of Finnish Lapland, Rovaniemi, which could only be reached from that direction via the 480 kilometer long Arctic Highway. After capturing Petsamo, the 14th Army dispatched two regiments of its 104th Division south along the highway towards Rovaniemi, while the retreating Finns tried to gather sufficient forces to stop them.

Simultaneously, Rovaniemi faced amore imminent threat from the east, where the Soviet's 122nd Division was pushing westward along a much shorter road which led through the village of Salla and the railhead of Kemijarvi. When this division advanced across the border on 30 November, the only Finnish force within 150 kilometers was the 18th Separate Battalion. By 10 December, it had been forced to abandon Salla, the road to Kemijarvi was open, and the Russians were less than 105 kilometers from Rovaniemi.

Separated from the Salla front by more than 160 kilometers of woods and lakes, other columns of the 9th

Army were also advancing toward the Gulf of Bothnia. The 163rd Division was moving along the newly built road from Uhtua and crossed the Finnish border at Juntusranta where a reinforced Finnish platoon began its delaying action, withdrawing toward the village of Suomussalmi. A regimental combat team from the 163rd Division was advancing westward along a parallel road some 50 kilometers south of the Juntusranta road and crossed the border at Raate where two Finnish platoons were delaying its movement. These meager forces were reinforced by elements of the 15th Separate Battalion and a few days later by the 4th Field Replacement Battalion which was rushed there from Kajaani. On 7 December the two columns of the Soviet 163rd Division joined and captured the Suomussalmi Village. Now the entire division was ready to continue to its objective, the city of Oulu, only 240 kilometers to the west by road.

About 90 kilometers southeast of Suomussalmi, a third element of the 9th Army was moving northwest along two roads from its base at Repola where the Finnish rail net was in places less than 80 kilometers from the frontier. The immediate objective of this column which was formed of elements of the Soviet 54th Division was the village of Kuhmo. Along this road, the Finnish 14th Separate Battalion was delaying the enemy. These pitifully weak screening forces opposing the Soviet 9th Army's three separate columns used the scorched earth policy to slow down the intruders while the few roads were clogged with civilians fleeing from their homes with their infants, cattle and few belongings in sub-zero cold.

The Soviet 8th Army operating in the region known as Ladogan-Karelia directly north of Lake Ladoga used more concerted tactics than the 9th Army in the north. Its thrusts came dangerously close to communications and population centers of southern Finland and the rear of the Finnish Karelian Isthmus Army's positions. There the

Finnish IV Corps' screening and covering forces consisting initially of three separate battalions and later five additional battalions from the 12th and 13th Finnish Divisions found themselves too weak to stop the overwhelmingly strong Soviet forces along the preplanned zones within the 100 kilometer wide sector. Consequently, the Soviet 8th Army's five separate attack columns were advancing almost at will toward their objective, the Sortavala-Joensuu railroad, before they were stopped between Pitkaranta and Sortavala, and at Kollaa, Tolvajarvi and Ilomantsi.

Finnish screening and covering forces had no better luck either in the Karelian Isthmus. Onto the relatively narrow bridge linking Leningrad directly with the heart of southern Finland, the enemy threw his major forces, eight infantry divisions and five armored brigades of the 7th Army. Anticipating that the major blow would fall on the Isthmus, the Finnish army had concentrated its main force there, five front line divisions. In front of these forces were the four separate groups with screening and covering missions as previously explained. After an intensive half hour barrage by some 600 artillery guns at 0700 hours, 30 November, the intended blitzkrieg assault was launched along the entire Karelian Isthmus frontier. Near the Gulf of Finland, the Soviet 70th Division captured some of the border guards, and by nightfall it had pushed the U group's border guard companies back to the Terijoki-Joutselka road line where the group was planning to stop the advance by employing the 1st Jaeger battalion and one of the Civil Guard battalions. However, the adjacent M group withdrew even faster, falling back as far as the vicinity of Bamppala, and by the late afternoon of 2 December, the U group commander had no other choice but to order further withdrawal of his forces.

Farther north in the center of the Isthmus, the Red Army encountered stubborn house to house fighting at Lipola village on 30 November, but that covering group, too, had to withdraw much faster than originally planned.

Near Lake Ladoga, the Soviets captured the village of Metsapirtti during the first night. The successful Soviet regiment was supported by heavy tanks, seldom used at this stage of the war. The counterattack conducted by the R group on 2 December failed to dislodge the Russians, and by the next day the Soviets were in front of Lake Suvanto, the easternmost part of the Vuoksi River, and the Taipale River.

Due to the width of the U group zone and the excellent terrain for mass employment of tanks, the light Finnish forces were in danger of becoming cut off from their lines of communications. Having lost all of their anti-tank weapons, these widely scattered company and cavalry escadron (escadrill)-size units were too vulnerable for fast moving tanks.

As the rapid withdrawal continued, Marshal Mannerheim expressed his dissatisfaction to the Isthmus army commander on 4 December. All field commanders, however, felt that since the Mannerheim Line had already been occupied by the field army forces, a more stubborn defense of the forward zone at the risk of heavy casualties was unwarranted. Marshal Mannerheim, on the other hand, wanted the covering forces to maintain the most effective possible defense much closer to the border region, utilizing forces large enough to inflict heavy losses on the enemy, while taking maximum advantage of the field works constructed during the past years there. As a result of Marshal Mannerheim's directive to the Isthmus Army commander on 3 December, the covering forces offered stronger resistance during the last days of their mission.

On the 6th, however, the Soviet right wing managed to cross the Taipale River and seize a strongpoint at Koukunniemi. The attackers suffered heavy casualties in this engagement; they had to fight off ten Finnish counterattacks that night. The Koukkuniemi positions were situated on the lowland meadows within the horseshoe bend of the river, exposed to highly effective fire from the main Finnish positions on the commanding heights.

By 6 December, all of the weary covering troops had been withdrawn through the main positions on the Mannerheim Line. The defeats and demoralization during this first week of the war were almost always caused by the appearance of Soviet tanks which rumbled through the frontier zone by the score. The relentless approach of these mechanical monsters, spewing deadly fire from the mouths of their cannon and machine guns, created in the infantrymen armed with only a rifle, a sense of desperation and terror. The Swedish made Bofors 37mm anti-tank guns, mostly assigned to the Isthmus Army units, were quite effective against the light T-26 tanks generally used by the Russians in the December fighting. However, these guns were much too few, and too heavy to move by men in the changing situations of mobile warfare. Although 80 tanks were knocked out by the Bofors guns and the regular artillery guns by 5 December and many others were destroyed by mines, their replacements appeared inexhaustible to the covering troops. The simpler weapon, the "Molotov cocktail" was not practicable under the fast moving situations on open terrain.

As the first week of war came to a close, there was an air of apprehension at Marshal Mannerheim's Headquarters in Mikkeli. The enemy was still advancing in force along the entire eastern border region, and Finnish troops were on the verge of collapse at several widely separated points. At the same time, Soviet leaders, knowing the vast superiority of their weapons and manpower resources, were so optimistic that they issued orders not to violate the Swedish neutrality while reaching her borders.

The Battle of Summa (17-20 December 1939)

From the first two weeks' activity of the Soviet forces on the Karelian Isthmus front, it became clear that they contemplated a two sided attack; one directed at Summa (in the Lahde area), the Viipuri gateway, and the other toward Taipale on the extreme eastern end of the Mannerheim Line. Obviously the Summa-Lahde area as the primary objective was of crucial importance for both sides because, if the attack succeeded, it would open the road to Viipuri and Helsinki and the Finnish heartland, thus bringing an end to the war by crushing the majority of the Finnish forces in a large pincer movement.

The Soviet 7th Army attacks in the Taipale region near Lake Ladoga were obviously a diversion intended to draw Finnish reserves away from the main objective. The one Russian infantry division already there had been joined by a second, along with more artillery. The attack early in the morning of 15 December was repulsed. When the battle ended, the Russians had been driven back with a loss of 12 tanks and innumerable casualties.

As early as 9 December, the Isthmus Army G-2 alerted his counterpart in the 5th Division staff about the expected offensive against the forces defending the Muolaanjarvi Lake-Summajoki River gap. Subsequently, the 1st Brigade which had been the II Corps' reserve force was alerted for deployment and ordered to occupy the Corps' eastern sector from the railroad on Lahde to MuolaanJarvi Lake. The 14th Infantry which had occupied that sector from the beginning of the war was pulled back and attached to the 1st Division, the parent organization of the 1st Brigade.

Beginning 12 December, enemy probing attacks conducted by a battalion size force supported by a battalion of tanks, plus or minus, were carried out sector by sector along the Summa-Lahde sectors. The intensity of the artillery preparations for these attacks increased daily as more artillery was brought closer to the Mannerheim Line.

The anticipated offensive began on 17 December with an ear splitting crash of exploding bombs released by the supporting air arm. The large scale infantry and tank attacks were first concentrated against the Lahde sector defended by the 1st Battalion, 15th Infantry. Thirty five enemy tanks penetrated the front line at the point along the Lahde Road between the battalion's 1st and 2nd company sectors. Eight tanks advanced up to the battalion command post bunker and sealed it off. Fortunately, the battalion commander had just departed and was on his way toward the battalion left flank. The battle against the tanks continued all day long; 22 of them were destroyed by explosive charges and "Molotov cocktails." Several tanks were made immobile by placing heavy logs between the treads and the wheels. The battalion commander, Captain Kuiri, was given credit for making four enemy tanks immobile.

By 2000 hours, the enemy's first echelon assault units had penetrated two strongpoints. All the counterattacks conducted during the night had failed and the Russians were bringing in more troops under the cover of darkness. Early in the morning the salient was sealed off and the surrounded enemy units were subjected to heavy losses.

On 19 December, 12 enemy tanks drove again into the battalion sector by following immediately the supporting artillery's barrages; also some infantry elements followed the tanks. A new, deep penetration up to the battalion support line made the situation very critical. A field artillery gun was placed into an anti-tank role and it destroyed most of the enemy tanks which were roaming around aimlessly without infantry support. The lack of cooperation and coordination between the armor force and the assaulting infantry caused the enemy a failure in his first real attempt.

During the night of 20 December, a third Soviet assault was directed into that part of the battalion's sector which included one of the recently built modern concrete bunkers named "Poppius" after Lieutenant Poppius, the strongpoint commander. During the latest attack on his sector, two enemy tanks . "parked" themselves in front of the two machine gun firing apertures, thus neutralizing the bunkers' fire power and also causing the bunker's defenders to abandon it. A counterattack that night, however, was successful and all the battalion forward positions were again regained. Small skirmishes against the sealed off enemy detachments continued until the following night. Losses among both Finnish and Russian units were heavy.

Also on 17 December, a massive effort was made to penetrate the Finnish positions at Summa village. Wave after wave of Russian troops were sent against the Finnish positions all along the Summa village sector. All infantry and tank penetrations, however, were repulsed that night.

On the 18th, an even larger tank battle was being conducted on the Summa village front. During the afternoon, a heavy tank battalion penetrated the line while lighter tanks restricted their support by staying with the infantry. The light tanks were equipped with flame throwers and caused numerous casualties among the defenders. Of the total number of tanks participating in the attack, 25 were destroyed and the commander of the heavy tank battalion was captured. The Finnish anti-tank company's 37mm guns destroyed about a dozen of the light tanks before being destroyed themselves by the Russian direct fire artillery. Some forward defense

positions were lost temporarily but the entire defense system was in friendly hands on the morning of the 19th.
Irrespective of their losses, the Russians renewed their attacks on Summa village on the following day after a 3 hour artillery preparation. The rolling barrages covered large areas from the front line up to the regimental support line about three kilometers in depth. About 80 tanks were used again in the assault. Ten tanks were knocked out by the Finnish artillery before the infantry assault began; about one-half of the tanks which penetrated the line were destroyed, again by individual tank destroyers or two man teams using from three to six kg explosive charges. The unexpected loss of tanks and heavy casualties among the assaulting infantry caused the Russian command to halt the offensive on 20 December. The Russian artillery, however, continued to fire upon the Finnish positions and lines of communications to the rear throughout the night. This kept the already battle fatigued defenders in front line positions without sleep or rest, and many soldiers even without food, for over 36 hours. During the battle, almost all Finnish telephone lines were cut which made the situation very dangerous. Messenger communications were the only relatively reliable means for the commanders to direct the operations within a battalion. Communications from the regiment to the battalions were kept primarily via artillery radio nets. Mortar companies' telephonic communications were often times disrupted during the most critical periods of a battle causing the company commanders to fire the most important targets at random or based on the information obtained through messengers.
During the four day battle of Summa and Lahde, there were hundreds of tanks operating at any one time; 58 of them never returned to their staging areas, how many did return but were damaged, no one knows. Twelve of the

slightly damaged tanks needed only minor repairs and were evacuated by the Finns.

In other sectors east of Summa, the Red Army did no better. On the Munasuo sector, the Russian tanks found themselves in such a thick forest that they could not leave the road and were forced to proceed almost literally into the killing zone of the Finnish artillery in a tight formation. Consequently, they suffered heavy losses and were forced to turn around and withdraw the following day.

The Red Army continued the attack with a constant supply of fresh troops to replace the casualties, and new tanks to replace those which did not return to their own staging areas. However, despite all efforts to make a breakthrough on the Summa front, the front line positions were in friendly hands all along the 5th Division's sector in the morning of 21 December. The situation was the same all along the Karelian Isthmus.

The battle of Summa taught the Finns that the tank traps were much too low, especially in the winter; in addition, they were too far out in front of the firing positions. It was difficult to keep the traps under surveillance, thus allowing the enemy to conceal its advance under restricted visibility conditions. It was noticed that the sleeping and rest bunkers were too far away from the firing positions, and that they did not provide adequate cover against artillery fire. In many cases, the trench systems had long straight sections which made it easy for enemy tanks to keep large sections under fire and thus allow the assaulting infantry to penetrate the line.

When the grand battle on the Summa-Lahde front was over, Finnish troops had destroyed 239 tanks on the Isthmus alone.

Finnish Forces' Offensive in December

("SA-kuva" - "Finnish Armed Forces photograph" in Finnish.)

General Ohquist, the II Corps Commander had requested permission for a counteroffensive with his II Corps forces before the Soviet 7th Army could deploy additional fresh forces opposite his corps. He had revised an earlier plan which had been disapproved by Marshal Mannerheim as too risky. Now the new plan which reached the general headquarters around noon on 22 December, only 18 hours from the H-hour, was approved.

The plan outlined a major offensive on a front of approximately 40 km, from Kuolemanjarvi Lake to Muolaanjarvi Lake. According to the plan, the 6th Division, which was in reserve behind Summa, reinforced by an infantry regiment, was to join parts of other II Corps divisions in the offensive. On the right, parts of the 4th Division were to advance on the right flank of the spearheading 6th Division, which was to attack along the Summa River. Parts of the 5th Division which was defending the front line at Summa would be responsible for tying down the enemy forces in the vicinity of Summa. On the left, groups from the 1st Division were to attack along the railroad, white further left, parts of the 11th Division were to advance south and then westward to penetrate the Russian forces' positions, tie them down and secure the left flank of the main effort forces.

The general offensive was scheduled to begin at 0630 hours on 23 December, but many units were late in reaching their attack positions due to inadequate planning and reconnaissance. Some of the supporting artillery units did not even reach their firing positions until the afternoon. Artillery coordination was poor, partly due to inadequate knowledge of enemy dispositions, but especially because of poor communications with the advancing infantry. The lack of reliable radio equipment was once again the main reason for the failure. General Ohquist even lost contact with two of his divisions. These same factors caused the dispersal of the attack formations, which soon fragmented into isolated battalions and companies waging their own separate infantry battles. The attack forces gained only about 3-4 kilometers before stiff enemy resistance halted their advance. The 6th Division had the worst luck of all the II Corps' forces. In a relatively open country, its forces were vulnerable to enemy machine gun and artillery fire; the latter were exceptionally accurate because it was directed from two captive balloons. It also appeared that strong Russian forces had been grouped for an attack there when the 6th Division advance forces advanced.

Those units which had carried a reasonably heavy burden in defeating the Russians less than two days earlier were in no way in shape, physically or psychologically, for a counterattack in deep snow and cold weather conditions. Many of the participating men had had hardly four hours sleep since the end of the Russian offensive. A lack of adequate artillery and mortar ammunition prevented the conduct of any preparation fires prior to the attack. Due to seasonable cold weather, a large percentage of the 81mm mortar rounds did not explode. In addition, the resupply of ammunition was almost impossible during the attack. No horse drawn vehicles could follow the troops in daylight over wide fields of open terrain; furthermore, there were no covered roads into the objective area. This same condition badly hampered the evacuation of casualties; consequently, too much manpower was needed for hauling the wounded in ahkios (a type of toboggan or sledge without runners). Finally, a lack of anti-tank weapons was a critical problem within the objective areas where the Russian forces defended themselves by using tanks to defend their circular perimeters. For this reason alone, the Finns could not even get close enough to the enemy to destroy them in close combat. The attack was made on too wide a front without any real concentration of forces along the primary zone of attack.

After eight hours, General Ohquist ordered the attack halted and the Finns withdrew to their own lines without interference. Fortunately, the enemy was also stunned about the unexpected Finnish offensive and was not prepared for a rapid countermove.

Russian casualties must have been considerable. In one isolated battle, a Russian combat engineer unit was surprised by a superior Finnish force which caused the enemy heavy casualties. When those Finnish troops were withdrawing, they surrounded a Russian battalion which was rescued by another Russian unit's counterattack.

Although the counterattack was hardly a success, it improved the morale of the troops and, perhaps more importantly, it shook up the Russians. The abortive attack may have had one positive result, the Russians made no effort to renew their large scale attacks on the Isthmus for a month, except for sporadic sorties at Taipale from 25 to 27 December and minor skirmishes along the entire Mannerheim Line in January 1940.

Russian Preparation for a New Offensive on the Isthmus

Reorganization of Forces and a New Strategy. After suffering stunning defeats on the Karelian Isthmus during December, the Red Army "licked its wounds" and, at the same time, looked for ways to improve its performance. It is apparent that Stalin himself undertook a reappraisal of the situation. He dismissed his Commissar for Defense, Marshal Voroshilov and appointed Timoshenko to replace him and also made Marshal Timoshenko Commander-in-Chief of the Red forces operating on the Finnish theater of operations. Stalin revised the strategy of these forces by calling for greater concentration of forces and a new effort on the Karelian Isthmus, and more cautious "adventures" on the northern fronts.

Although it had been expected that the Russians would immediately prepare for and launch a new offensive to restore their prestige, they spent the month of January primarily for conducting reconnoitering attacks and destroying Finnish strong points, especially the concrete bunkers on the Summa-Lahde front by heavy 8-11" artillery from direct-fire positions only a few hundred meters away. They also pinpointed Finnish artillery emplacements by using aerial balloons as observation points and kept them under constant harassing fires. Also the Red Air Force increased its activities against targets in the immediate vicinity of the front line. Due to artillery and air activity, it was almost impossible to bring supplies up to the front and evacuate casualties during daylight hours. Therefore, troops received one hot meal a day which was carried in containers during darkness. These same horse drawn sleds were used for evacuating casualties to the rear. In spite of the extreme cold weather, "korsus" (dugouts), tents or other types of shelters could not be heated during daylight hours; even a trace of smoke invited artillery and mortar fire, even air bombardment.

During the month of January, the Red Army was reinforced up to overwhelming strength. Also a reorganization of troops was ordered. The group of divisions which had been fighting in the eastern zone of the Isthmus was transformed into the 13th Army. The 7th Army, originally deployed in the entire Isthmus zone, was assigned the new breakthrough mission along the Summa-Lahde gateway to Viipuri.

Intensive Training and Innovations.

All Red Army forces underwent intensive training behind the lines, and those army corps assigned the breakthrough role practiced their operations against a simulated "Mannerheim Line" with actual replicas of the Finnish concrete bunkers built behind the lines. The probing attacks conducted against Finnish troops on various sectors in January were clearly better organized and led than those of December.

During the attacks conducted in early January, even some new innovations were battle tested. For example, armor plated troop carrying sleds, some equipped with machine guns, were either pushed by tanks or towed behind them. A sled could carry a squad of men. Flame throwing tanks were used to burn the defenders in trenches. This tactic was tested already in the first battle of Summa in December. Individual shields mounted on skis were used to provide riflemen cover, concealment and protection while they advanced by crawling in deep snow. Such a technique was frequently used by engineer patrols for bringing explosive charges forward to the tank obstacles (boulder traps) for the purpose of clearing gaps for the advancing tanks.

Infantry and tank teams practiced coordinated attacks, and tanks also learned to support each other more closely which made it increasingly difficult and dangerous for Finnish tank destroyer teams or individual men to employ explosive charges and "Molotov cocktails" against tanks, especially in daylight. The few Finnish anti-tank guns, most of them antiquated models, were not able to cope with all of the tank attack formations, which at times included as many as 100-150 tanks. An example of a poorly coordinated tank assault took place at Summa front during 17-19 December when a heavy tank battalion penetrated along the Finnish positions and was doomed to be destroyed during darkness because the lighter tanks and infantry were stopped in front of the Finnish line.

Improvement of Morale and Political Indoctrination of Troops.

While the reorganization was going on, vast quantities of supplies, ammunition and equipment were transported into the tactical units' rear positions. In addition, communication networks on the Isthmus were extended and improved. Troop morale was also a concern for the new leadership. Several high ranking political officers were brought in and political indoctrination classes were increased underlining patriotism and the soldiers' duty to "destroy the enemy forces and thus forever prevent the Finnish warmongers' access to the Gulf of Finland" as the

7th Army commander addressed his troops in his order of the day on 30 November 1939, the first day of the war.

Kuusinen's Army.

The puppet "Terijoki government" headed by Mr. Kuusinen, a former Finn who had escaped to Russia during the Finnish war of independence and became a trustee of Stalin, even had its own army. The "First Finnish Corps" of volunteers, the alleged nucleus of a future "People's Army of Finland," had, in accordance with the Red Star (a Soviet Army newspaper), some 5,000 men. The great majority of these men were recruited from those communists who fled Finland in 1918 and from Finnish speaking East Karelian Ingermanlanders. Only a handful of Finnish POW's are known to have signed themselves up in the "Kuusinen's Corps." The Soviet psychological warfare measures were totally unsuccessful in their effort to influence Finnish soldiers for desertion.

Soviet Propaganda.

Soviet propagandists were so misinformed that they promised the Finnish soldiers an eight hour work day in the future Soviet Finland, something which had been in force in Finland for two decades. A vast shower of leaflets, radio broadcasts and loudspeaker appeals to front line troops failed to convince them that life was better in the Soviet Union or that Finland's defeat was imminent. These two themes were primarily used for propagandizing Finnish soldiers.

Red Army's February Offensive

Deployment of forces in the Karelian Isthmus was as follows:

Finnish Army of Karelia: Lieutenant General H. Osterman (later Lieutenant General E. Heinrichs)

a. II Corps: Lieutenant General H. Ohquist
b. III Corps: Major General E. Heinrichs (later Major General P. Talvela)
c. Reserve.

Red Army:
a. 7th Army
b. 13th Army.

Operations.

Both Red armies started to conduct probing attacks on the entire length of their respective zones on 1 February. Apparently the purpose was to mislead the Finnish commanders and to wear out the defenders whose ranks were diminishing at a dangerous rate. Steady artillery and mortar fires plus repeated air attacks continued many times a day and night kept all awake and alert for an expected attack. At the same time, the Russians rotated fresh units to the front for every significant mission. The battle fatigue caused many Finnish soldiers to become completely apathetic. They were falling asleep even during combat.

The strongest attacks were made against the 3rd Division in the Sumna front, and at Taipale. On 1 February, three of the concrete bunkers which were the bastions of the strongpoints, were partially eliminated out of action; one surrounded by tanks and infantry, the other two partially destroyed by artillery fire. The surrounded one, however, was retaken during the following night by elements of local Finnish reserves.

Attack patterns.

There were certain patterns to the operations, although their timing, intensity and location varied considerably. Always, first came a strong artillery preparation accompanied by aerial bombardment. Artillery preparation included wide and deep area fires on the entire front lasting from one half to five hours and including areas up to tactical reserve locations.

About 30 minutes prior to the H-hour, preparatory fires were concentrated on defensive installations, command posts, artillery and mortar fire positions, tactical reserves, etc. The last concentration was normally on the penetration point. Russian tanks advanced sometimes within their own barrage, at least the first tanks moved forward only a few seconds after the last artillery rounds. Immediately prior to the attack, mortar fires were switched on the penetration point(s) to neutralize the defenders. Often the first attack echelon advanced through their own fires. All fires were laid down with such weight and volume, and many times also with accuracy, that tanks and infantry were able to "drive and walk" into the initial Finnish positions without opposition.

Very seldom did the Russian infantry attack without tank support. The tank obstacles generally were found in front of defensive positions all along the Mannerheim Line which hindered and slowed down tank movements in support of an infantry attack. Therefore, open passages through the obstacles were required. These were made either by using explosives or by direct artillery fire. A lack of anti-tank weapons on the Finnish side allowed the Russian tank formations to advance almost at will, even to move parallel with the Finnish defense lines for the purpose of destroying crew served weapons positions or burning the trench system and personnel with flamethrowers.

Infantry onslaughts supported by large numbers of tanks were often repeated three or more times a day on a narrow front (normally 1-3 kilometers) with fresh troops committed to each wave. On a division sector, like the Summa-Lahde-Merkki front of about 15 kilometers wide,

three divisions and a tank brigade were employed offensively, while a fourth division served as a back up force. This size of force, often supported by 200 aircraft, could attack four times a day. A fresh force was often thrown into action the very next day.
Under these conditions, the regular field artillery became increasingly critical to the defense. Unfortunately, Finnish forces' ammunition reserves were already at the end of January so short that commanders were forced to place more strict limits to the use of artillery. Only absolutely essential targets could be engaged. This meant that the Russian troops, especially their artillery and other support units did not need to worry about being "disturbed" within their bivouac areas. By comparison, the Russian commanders could afford the luxury of expending tens of thousands of artillery ammunition during preparatory fire as well as for the harassing fires during the in between period. Furthermore, Red aircraft, roaming over the Finnish positions by the hundreds, attacked Finnish artillery units constantly, especially when they fired, thus restricting the use of artillery. Observation balloons were also used to direct Soviet artillery on Finnish artillery and mortar positions.

Marshal Timoshenko's Operational Plan and Its Execution

At the end of the first week of February 1940, the new operational plan for the Red Army seemed to become effective. Apparently, it called for a major thrust toward Viipuri on the zone Muolaanjarvi Lake-Summajarvi Lake-Summa Village, with a secondary drive toward Antrea Station from the Muolaanjarvi Lake-Vuoksi River front, and a third advance aimed at Kakisalmi from the Taipale Region at the eastern end of the Mannerheim Line.

Attack on Lahde Front Beginning on 11 February.

During the night of 10-11 February, the Russian assault units occupied their attack positions. Additional artillery intended for point blank firing was moved forward by hand in order not to alert the Finns. The day of February 11 was cold; the mercury dropped to about -25C, but by 0800 hours the Russian 123rd Division and the supporting 35th Tank Brigade were in their jumping off positions. The tanks were about 1-3 kilometers from the Finnish lines. About the same time, hundreds of artillery guns (over 50 batteries) blanketed their target areas, reaching deep into regimental support line areas. The entire Mannerheim Line was experiencing an unprecedented barrage of artillery fire. The preparation lasted for 2-3 hours.

The artillery fire in the Lahde Road sector was the most terrifying ever experienced. By the time this storm was over, several concrete bunkers were destroyed and other field fortifications were crushed, many like matchsticks.

Behind the two kilometer front between Summajarvi Lake and the Munasuo Swamp, there were five concrete bunkers, including the most modern, "Poppius," just west of the Lahde Road and the "Million" about one kilometer further westward by the Summajarvi Lake, each consisting of three machine guns, an artillery forward observer team and two to three rifle squads. Both of these bunkers and the three older model bunkers were extensively damaged before the massive barrage of 11 February. In addition to these permanent fortifications, there were a number of earth and timber machine gun nests and trench systems which also were destroyed by the preparatory fire.

To defend the entire two kilometer front, there was only an understrength battalion, the 2nd Battalion, 9th Infantry. Its three rifle companies were all on line: the 1st Company to the west occupying the second which included the "Million" bunker; the 2nd Company in the center occupying the Lahde Road sector which included the "Poppius" bunker; and the 3rd Company to the east occupying the Munasuo Swamp sector. The support line in this sector was located from 800 to 1,500 meters behind the forward positions.

While the other 18 divisions and five tank brigades were simultaneously engaged in the offensive across the entire Karelian Isthmus, the attack in the Lahde Road sector began at Noon, 11 February. The Russian 123rd Division commenced its well rehearsed assault on fortified positions with one regiment in reserve. One regiment attacked against the 1st Company's sector near the "Million" bunker, while the other regiment advanced against the 3rd Company's sector on the right. The center, the Lahde Road sector and its "Poppius" bunker, were attacked by a reinforced battalion supported by two companies of tanks. The defenders, however, delivered such effective fire from the damaged bunkers and the remaining trenches that they held up the advance of the attacker.

The second echelon of the attack regiment was committed to the battle while scores of tanks pounded the defenses at point blank range. In the furious fighting, four heavy tanks were damaged before the last anti-tank gun was smashed. At least one Russian infantry company lost all of its men in the assault. When tanks halted right in front of the embrasures of "Poppius" bunker, its crew finally abandoned that fortification to continue to battle in the open. In the eastern sector, the 3rd Company cut down the enemy infantry attacking across the Munasuo Swamp; but it was compelled to retreat later in the afternoon when T-28 tanks flanked it along the Lahde Road.

The battle for the "Million" bunker seesawed into the night. The Russians repeatedly surrounded it, only to be thrown back by counterattacks of the defenders. Within a few hours, the Finnish 2nd Battalion, 9th Infantry had lost one half of its manpower and most crew served weapons. Late in the afternoon, the survivors of the 2nd Battalion, 9th Infantry could not hold their positions any longer. By the time darkness fell, the Russian tanks and infantry had advanced up to the battalion support line along the Lahde Road where they dug in for the night.

Although Marshal Timoshenko's great 11 February offensive extended across the entire Karelian Isthmus, in no other sector was its success as great as at Lahde. At Summa, west of the Lahde Road penetration, strong attacks which began in the morning continued late into the night, but the 7th Infantry held its positions.

Elsewhere along the exhausted 3rd Division sector, the attackers took some forward positions at Merkki, the division's easternmost sector, but the defenders also recaptured these and beat back the renewed assaults that night.

West of the 3rd Division sector, the Russians penetrated the forward zone of the 4th Division sector two kilometers south of Marjapellonmaki around Noon, 11 February. Concurrently, the Russians also tried to flank the Division over the ice of the Gulf of Finland. Some 2-3 battalions of marines approached the coast behind the Mannerheim Line near Muurila. Local coastal batteries caused the attackers to stop and spread out for the time being.

On the opposite flank of the 3rd Division in the Taasionlampi-Suursuo Swamp area, the 1st Division met strong Russian forces supported by about a battalion of tanks. However, these became stuck in the partially frozen marsh and the offensive lost its momentum.

It had been a demanding day for the front line unit commanders of the 3rd Division, for the II Corps commander and no less for the Commanding General of the Karelian Isthmus Army, General Osterman. During the evening, however, elements of the 8th Infantry Regiment succeeded in clearing the enemy out of the western part of the Lahde Road sector, and two battalions continued the counterattack along the Lahde Road in an attempt to regain the eastern portion of the badly beaten 2nd Battalion, 9th Infantry.

Marshal Mannerheim Releases His Reserves.

Late at night on 11 February, Marshal Mannerheim became convinced that local reserves had been used to their maximum capacity and that his own reserves must be employed to save the extremely critical situation. Accordingly, he released his main reserve force, the 5th Division, to the use of the II Corps' commander. (The 5th Division included the 13th Infantry, the 14th Infantry and the 15th Infantry regiments.) The 15th Infantry was initially attached to the 4th Division on the west, while the 13th Infantry was ordered to occupy the support line at the Lahde Road sector.

General Ohquist, the II Corps Commander was put into a difficult situation. He knew that his western flank, the 4th Division sector was in danger of becoming outflanked by forces advancing over the ice on the Gulf and that there were penetrations on the Marjapellonmaki area. He also recognized the even greater threat at Lahde, east of the Summa front. In order to be prepared for this latter threat, he decided to neutralize the first of the danger spots within the 4th Division sector by dispatching one half of the 15th Infantry into his western flank with the mission of assisting the 4th Division commander in recapturing the pockets near Marjapellonmaki-Muurila coastal areas threatened by the enemy forces advancing across the ice. The other half of the 15th Infantry was temporarily attached to the 3rd Division for the purpose of clearing the enemy penetrations at Suokanta in the westernmost sector of the division.

A battalion combat team consisting of the 1st Battalion, 15th Infantry and the Mortar Company, 15th Infantry was alerted on 10 February and ordered to march cross country from Naykkijarvi Lake area to a position within the 4th Division sector. Its mission was to be prepared to conduct combat operations as directed by the 4th Division Commander. Upon arrival at the objective area after a 25 kilometer march off roads, the combat team received another mission:

"The 1st Battalion will march as soon as possible to the Suokauta sector and be prepared to counterattack and regain the positions now in enemy hands." This meant another 15 kilometers without rest or food within the last 24 hours. In the meantime, the mortar company was ordered to continue to the Lahde sector and be prepared there to support the 13th Infantry within that sector. The distance to the objective area was about 25 kilometers. It was a clear, cold night with temperatures of -30C. The mortar company arrived at Majakyla bridge at 0300 hours, 13 February. Upon receipt of its mission from the commander of the 13th Infantry, the company participated in the Lahde campaign providing the various battalions of the 13th Infantry fire support until late evening of 15 February.

At that time, advancing Soviet forces threatened to overrun the company positions and the company was given the order to march to a location about 10 kilometers northwest and on arrival to report to his commanding officer, the CO, 15th Infantry, for further assignment. This was a typical example of a situation when commanders were tempted to employ even strategic reserves in a piece meal fashion to satisfy too many urgent needs of subordinate commands.

The Last Campaign on Summa-Lahde Sectors and on V-Line

1-12 February 1940. While the 123rd Soviet Division continued its attack to widen the base of its wedge along the Lahde Road zone, the second echelon regiment which was clearing the few remaining Finnish pockets along the forward edge of the battle area was halted by the 1st Company, 9th Infantry. Its platoon still occupied the "Million" bunker strongpoint. Fierce seesaw battles raged around the severely damaged fort all afternoon and into the night of the 11th when Russian infantry finally surrounded it for the last time. Under cover of darkness, a Soviet sapper group of combat engineers hauled in a tank drawn sled and a great amount of explosives and positioned them on the bunker in the early hours of the 12th and detonated them. An ear splitting explosion blasted a 10 meter crater in the fortification and killed the entire Finnish platoon. Regardless of the crippling loss, the 1st Company, 9th Infantry held their totally isolated positions until Noon, when they withdrew north of Summajarvi Lake to the battalion support line.

Although there was some fierce fighting at the Lahde Road support line on 12 February, the Russian 123rd Division seemed to consolidate its gain rather than continuing the offensive. This hesitation on the part of the Russian 7th Army gave the Finnish forces a short but very important breathing spell. During the pause, Finnish reserves were brought from their distant staging areas toward the Lahde Road sector, and plans for counteroffensives were formulated.

The major counterattacks for the morning of 12 February were to be a three pronged strike to recapture the front line. At 0700 hours, two battalions of the 14th Infantry began their attacks by advancing from the Majakyla Village along the western side of the Majajoki River with the mission to attack in a southeasterly direction on the left flank of the Russian 123rd Division which was consolidating its gains on the 1 kilometer wide salient. By noon, the counterattacking force had thrown the enemy's elements within its zone off the hill north of Summajarvi Lane. The advance came, however, to its inevitable halt when the enemy's overwhelmingly superior artillery was directed against the Finnish battalion (lst Battalion, 14th Infantry).

During this phase of the counteroffensive, the leading battalion changed its commander four times in an hour. During the afternoon, tanks smashed through the battalion forcing the regimental commander to order a withdrawal to the support line between Suursuo Swamp and Majajoki River. The eastern part of this line was manned by the remnants of the 9th Infantry, reinforced by a battalion from the 13th Infantry. Losses were especially heavy among the officers, even the regimental commander was mortally wounded early on the morning of 13 February.

Elements of the 3rd Brigade were counterattacking from the east against the right flank of the Russian 123rd Division. For an unknown reason, the attack was delayed and the Russians were able to stop it in front of their temporary defense line which secured their eastern flank.

13-14 February.

The 13th Infantry which was defending on and behind the support line was under extreme pressure early on the morning of the 13th. Good flying weather facilitated the heaviest air attacks to date, and artillery fire was intensive. In the morning, several attacks were repulsed but in the afternoon some 50 tanks broke through just east of the Lahde Road on a front about 800 meters wide. Since there were no anti-tank guns available, there was little hope of preventing the Russian 123rd Division and

its supporting 35th Tank Brigade from exploiting their success.
The fighting at the point of the breakthrough was so fierce that in one company with a strength of more than 100, only 14 survived. Due to the confusion of those hectic moments, the Finnish infantry neglected to warn the artillery about the Russian tanks' penetration and ten 152mm howitzers of the supporting artillery battalion were abandoned when heavy tanks overran their positions east of Majakyla Village. The last tank destroyer unit in the II Corps was rushed to the area but just when these men were preparing for their suicidal attacks in the evening, additional tanks overran them. This time, Soviet infantry accompanied the armor by riding on the tanks up to the next Finnish position and protected them. The massive tank onslaught was terrifying. It is understandable that some of the helpless defenders fled in panic, while other reserves were being rushed to the scene. The gloomy situation, however, took another turn; incredibly, the Russian spearhead suddenly halted its advance at night after a promising two kilometer deep penetration.
Although the Finns had no more fresh reserves, another counterattack was being planned for the night of 13-14 February to dislodge the enemy from its positions along the line about 1,200 meters south of the Majakyla-Lahde crossroad. However, the plan was cancelled late at night. The critical shortage of artillery ammunition led to the realization that sending troops against tanks on the reasonably open terrain where scores of tanks were maneuvering, would only lead to pointless slaughter.
The II Corps' last reserve, the Civil Guard battalion of young 13-15 year old school boys from Viipuri was employed together with the remnants of the 14th Infantry on the hastily organized line southeast of Majakyla. Elements of the 13th Infantry were occupying the

Majajoki River line, their front toward the east, while the 3rd Brigade was still covering the long eastern side of the Russian salient. In the meantime, the II Corps commander was organizing forces to man the next prepared positions along the so called V-line at Naykkijarvi Lake about 12 kilometers to the northwest.

High Level Conference on Future Operations.

A meeting was held at II Corps Headquarters on the morning of 14 February. It was attended by Marshal Mannerheim and Colonel Airo, the Marshal's right hand for plans and operations. Lieutenant General Osterman, the Isthmus Army Commander, and his Chief of Staff, Colonel Tapola were also present. The Commander-in-Chief had made the long trip from Mikkeli by car, traveling during the hours of darkness to elude hostile aircraft. After a short discussion, all parties agreed that the II Corps' position as it was at the present time was critical and that a withdrawal to the immediate V-Line was mandatory. The III Corps, however, would further defend its positions on the Vuoksi River Line. Detailed plans for new troop dispositions were outlined which would facilitate as orderly a withdrawal as possible. Furthermore, plans for obtaining reserves from other fronts, training centers, etc., were formulated. The immediately available reserves were meager:

a. Two coastal defense battalions from the southern coast west of Viipuri.

b. An artillery battery from a training center in Ostrobothnia.

c. Two infantry regiments (the 67th and the 68th) of the recently organized 23rd Division which would be diverted from assignment to the IV Corps in the Ladogan Karelia. These regiments had been activated by utilizing captured weapons and other equipment. Their manpower came primarily from two sources: from wounded personnel on convalescent leave, and from training centers which had been training young men of 17 years of age and personnel who never had received military training because of physical or mental defects.

Many of these reinforcements were delayed, however, by the extensive Soviet air activities on roads, bridges and rail centers. Enemy bomber formations were so numerous over the Viipuri region that many convoys bringing supplies for the front line troops were being delayed by several hours.

Soviet 123rd Division Hesitates to Continue and Exploit the Situation.

On the Lahde sector along the thinly manned line, meager Finnish units consisting of young school boys and combat fatigued men of the 14th Infantry were still holding their positions; so did the units on the both sides of the salient on the Lahde Road ridge. The mortar company, 15th Infantry was still supporting the units holding the Russians at bay.

The Soviet 7th Army Commander Meretskov had an open road stretching before him. There were no prepared defensive positions nearer than the intermediate line, called V-Line at Naykkijarvi Lake. An open nearly treeless area which afforded no cover for the Finnish tank destroyer teams was perfect terrain for the 123rd Division and its 35th Tank Brigade to advance and exploit the penetration to a breakthrough into Viipuri and even further into the Finnish heartland.

Since total victory was apparently within his grasp, why didn't Comrade Meretskov take full advantage of this opportunity? He had at his disposal a special mobile group consisting of a great number of tanks, motorized infantry and engineers designed to exploit the breakthroughs. Yet even without those special forces, the 7th Army could have continued the offensive with excellent chances for success. But perhaps the Soviet commanders had learned to respect the Finns who were hastily improvising a defense with reserves from every conceivable source. Nowhere, except at the Lahde Road zone, did the great offensive of the Russian Northwestern Front achieve results commensurate with its tremendous expenditure of manpower and resources.

Withdrawal to the Intermediate V-Line.

At 0700 hours, 14 February, all units surrounding the Soviet wedge received permission from the 5th Division Headquarters that if their positions became untenable, they could withdraw to improvised positions about one kilometer further northwest.

Units started to evacuate their positions in early afternoon, leaving small detachments to maintain fire and deceive the enemy. On the Majajoki River Line, the 3rd Battalion, 13th Infantry refused to withdraw until forced to do so by the Russians.

The developments within the Lahde Road area also made it necessary to evacuate the Summa sector now in imminent danger of being outflanked by the Russians from the northeast. Summa's formidable defenses had held out through 70 days of almost constant attacks, artillery barrages and air bombardments. During the night of 14-15 February, the 15th Infantry abandoned the area to the enemy who had prematurely boasted of capture of Summa over radio Moscow.

A more threatening loss of ground took place at Lahde Road sector where the Soviet 7th Army finally decided to follow up the 123rd Division's success after keeping its overwhelmingly superior forces immobilized for over two days. Between them and the road junction which would have opened them access to several roads leading towards Viipuri were only remnants of the 14th Infantry Regiment with two tank destroyer platoons without anti-tank guns, and one of the youthful Civil Guard companies from Viipuri. In sub-zero weather, these cold and weary troops laid on the open snowy ground without any protection against the Russian tank and infantry weapons' fire.

Russian Offensive Begins.

In the afternoon of 15 February the fresh Soviet forces of the specially trained and equipped mobile group consisting of a tank brigade with supporting infantry and combat engineers, and designed to exploit breakthroughs, blasted their way through the thin Finnish line along the northern part of the Lahde Road ridge. Finnish losses were severe, especially among the boys from Viipuri. By that evening, the survivors were completely worn out from fatigue.

Once again, the road lay open before the 7th Army. Colonel Baranov's ' special brigade was opposed by only meager Finnish troops here and there on the Kamara Ridge. The road and rail junction at Kamara Station was defended by one battalion of the 62nd Infantry Regiment which had recently arrived from the III Corps' area. Having been activated just a few weeks earlier, the battalion lacked combat experience. Incredibly, the relatively invincible Soviet spearhead halted about 1,500 meters north of Lahde-Kamara road junction. The special group's tank unit commanders felt the same respect toward their adversaries as their colleagues in the 123rd Division. They lost the opportunity to encircle the Finnish battalion and, thereafter, to continue through the thinly manned V-Line.

Defense on the V-Line.

At 1550 hours on 15 February, Marshal Mannerheim finally authorized the entire II Corps to pull back into the V-Line. It was partially prepared and included some tank traps as well as barbed wire fences on the main avenues of approach. This line ran from the northern tip of Muolaanjarvi Lake westward to Naykkijarvi Lake and further westward to the Bay of Viipuri at Uuraansaari Island.

The 5th Division carried again the heaviest burden by defending the Naykkijarvi Lake sector through which the railroad and the best and shortest roads led to Viipuri.

Beginning on 16 February, the Soviet 7th Army belatedly attempted to employ its mobile special brigade to encircle the rear guard battalion of the Finnish 5th Division at the Kamara Station area while the battalion withdrew from Summa along the roads only some five kilometers west of the Kamara Station. Fortunately, Colonel Baranov's tanks did not dare to go westward to block the Summa-Viipuri road and its parallel roads leading to Naykkijarvi region which were full of convoys. The Mortar Company, 15th Infantry which withdrew from the Majajoki bridge positions cross country toward Naykkijarvi was at one point so close to the Soviet tanks that it had to halt and look for concealment in order not to be seen by the Russian tank crews who had stopped on an adjacent road.

By the morning of 17 February, virtually all the Finnish II Corps' troops from the Mannerheim Line reached the V-Line. The Russian divisions were almost on their heels and reached the vicinity of Naykkijarvi the same night. Because the V-Line was only about 6 to 12 kilometers behind the main positions of the Mannerheim Line at Summa-Lahde area, there was a risk that the momentum of the Soviet drive mght carry it through this line before the retreating Finnish forces could properly occupy their positions. Furthermore, there was a great danger that the 4th Division forces far away on the west would become cut off during their retreat. Both sides sustained heavy casualties in the confused fighting of these days.

In the week ending 17 February, the 5th Division alone lost nearly 800 men killed in action. The battalion of the 62nd Infantry which Colonel Baranov's armor overran enroute to Kamara Station was so severely shaken by that baptism of fire that it could only be reformed far beyond the V-Line positions. Other green units of elderly men and recently recovered wounded personnel received similar shocks during their first encounter with the Russian tanks.

The most critical battles were waged on the sector immediately east of Naykkijarvi Lake where parts of the 123rd Division and Colonel Baranov's tank brigade drove into a weak Finnish defensive position along a narrow ridge at Honkaniemi Station. Repeated counterattacks failed to dislodge the enemy who by 23 February had seriously bent the Finnish line. The II Corps commander felt that the penetration endangered the entire corps' sector. Therefore, a counterattack was planned to dislodge the enemy.

On the morning of 26 February, a counterattack was launched by employing the Finnish Army's only tank company which had 37mm guns in support of several understrength battalions of infantry. Five of the 7 ton Vickers tanks were destroyed immediately after their departure from their attack positions, one of the tanks refused to start in the cold morning and was saved, while the remaining seven, having had difficulties advancing in the deep snow, returned safely to their base. The counterattack failed and the Soviet wedge along the railroad was threatening the II Corps' lines of communications with Viipuri.

On 27 February, Marshal Mannerheim authorized the withdrawal of the Finnish forces engaged in operations on the V-Line to the rear positions along the T-Line which ran from the Viipuri Bay along the outskirts of the City of Viipuri to Tali and further eastward to Karisalmi,

Kuparsaari, and then to the Vuoksi River at Pollakkala. Thus the 12 day battle on the V-Line had served its purpose by giving the High Command a few more days to adjust to the new situation and to make plans for the last stand along the T-Line.

No less than 12 Soviet infantry divisions and five tank brigades were required to force the five understrength and worn out Finnish divisions to withdraw. The Red Army's steamroller tactics had succeeded at last in the crucial western half of the Karelian Isthmus. The Finnish forces' retreat, although a hasty withdrawal, was carried out in orderly, gradual steps. During this phase, the Soviet Command failed again to properly utilize the tremendous breakthrough capabilities of the 123rd Division and the special tank heavy group assigned to the 7th Army for exploiting successes.

The hour long artillery barrage on 28 February ploughed up the V-Line positions before the Soviet forces commenced their assaults; but the only Finns they encountered were small delaying forces in widely scattered positions. By 3 March, the Finnish forces' withdrawal was completed and the stage was set for the final act of the war.

Change of Command.

On 19 February 1940, Commander of the Isthmus Army, Lieutenant General H. Osterman resigned from his command "for health reasons" and the III Corps Commander, Major General E. Heinrichs was promoted to Lieutenant General to fill that key post. The victor of Tolvajarvi campaigns, Major General P. Talvela was transferred to take command of the III Corps. In connection with these personnel changes, an organization change was also put into effect. On 20 February, a new command, the I Corps, was created in the Central Isthmus between the II and III Corps. Consisting of the 1st and

2nd Divisions, its boundary with the III Corps ran from Lyykylanjarvi Lake, just east of Tali to the Perojoki River. Major General T. Laatikainen, Commander of the 1st Division, took over the new Corps on 25 February, and Colonel A. Martola took over the 1st Division. This reorganization enabled Lieutenant General H. Ohquist to concentrate exclusively on the defense of Viipuri and its vicinity where the crucial battles would soon be fought.

The Last Campaigns of the Winter War

When the 4th Division withdrew to the V-Line and the coastal batteries on the Island of Koivisto were abandoned, the Gulf of Viipuri began to play a key role in the defense of Viipuri. The Soviet 7th Army was now able to cross the frozen Gulf to outflank the Viipuri defenses from the southwest. Therefore, on 18 February the Isthmus Army assumed responsibility for the defense of the Gulf. In order to strengthen the two coastal defense battalions which were spread thinly from the city of Hamina to Sakkijarvi on the east, Marshal Mannerheim turned to the Swedish Volunteer Corps which had been training in North Finland for several weeks. Their commander, General Linder, a veteran of the Finnish War of Independence (1918), accepted the Marshal's suggestion on 19 February that the volunteers assume the major responsibility for the defense of the Salla Front in the Arctic. Beginning on 22 February, some 8,000 Swedes and 725 Norwegians relieved five Finnish infantry battalions and two artillery batteries of the Lapland Group commanded by Major General K. Wallenius. These units began their long journey to the Viipuri Gulf area. General Wallenius was also transferred to direct the Gulf defenses.

By 22 February, Soviet forces had already secured a foothold on Peisaari Island northwest of Koivisto, and were threatening Uuras Island near Viipuri.

Peace Negotiations Between Helsinki and Moscow.

With the stronger defensive positions that Viipuri offered, the Finnish high command hoped to hold the Russians at bay until the spring thaw would cause the Red Army to halt or at least to slow down its advance until the war would come to an end in one way or another. By this time, serious peace negotiations were in progress between Helsinki and Moscow. From the information received through the Finnish negotiators, it was clear, however, that the Kremlin was determined to take as much territory from Finland as possible. For this reason, the battle of Viipuri took on added importance to both sides.

The Battle of Viipuri.

Immediately in front of the city, the 3rd and 5th Divisions held a line from Karenmaenlahti Bay to Tammisuo. In this sector, the 7th Army's spearheads drew a wedge in the line at Huhtiala, directly south of the Kolikkoinmaki suburb on 2 March. They followed up this success the following day with a penetration into the Finnish positions, and pushed the forward elements of the 3rd Division behind their main line. At the Tammisuo sector, the forward Finnish positions were still holding.

On 4 March, the enemy attacked all along the front but without success. By that evening, however, there were signs that the line might not hold. Therefore, a battalion from the 3rd Division's reserve regiment was sent to reinforce the front line positions. Another reserve battalion was dispatched to the north shore of Viipuri Bay to support the coastal defense forces.

On 5 March, the 7th Army continued to storm the 3rd Division defenses, threatening for a moment to break the line at Lintumus by the Majalahti Bay. At Tammisuo, the 5th Division's sector, two enemy tank assaults were repulsed. During March 6, there was only slight activity on the whole Viipuri front, although the artillery barrages

continued with great intensity. Only a minor assault at Lintumus had to be repulsed.
On 7 March, a small penetration was made at Huhtiala. Because the 3rd Division forces were unable to seal the gaps, the matter became critical by the 8th, and almost all reserves available to the II Corps were sent into combat. Also at this time, every available reserve unit from the I Corps area was on its way to the Viipuri area. Forces of the 5th Division were holding their positions intact, although counterattacks by local units were routine functions every night.
On 10 March, the Isthmus Army Commander decided that the 3rd Division's line should be shortened by a withdrawal to the immediate edge of the city. However, the order to withdraw was suspended for the time being. On the 11th, two more penetrations were made in the 3rd Division's sector and permission was given to execute the earlier order. At this point, Marshal Mannerheim intervened and ordered the 3rd Division to hold the line where it was, at least until the following evening. That order was based on "foreign policy matters." The negotiations for peace were nearing their final stages.
During the night of 11 March, the 7th Army broke the Finnish lines between Kesamaa and Porkka Island, southwest of Viipuri at the point between the 3rd Division and the Coast Group sectors. This major penetration posed such a threat to the whole defense system that General Ohquist, Commander of the II Corps, considered ordering withdrawal. A reserve consisting of two understrength companies, however, was found and sent to reinforce the forces along the perimeter of the bulge. The line held.
In the morning of 12 March, the 7th Army commenced its heaviest attack yet all along the lines of the 3rd and 5th Divisions. By that night, a number of large penetrations had been made in the Finnish lines between Karjala

Suburb and Tammisuo, but there was no possibility of a counterattack. The exhausted men were barely able to hold their positions around the gaps. At the point of the largest rupture near Tammisuo, the Russians proceeded to expand the gap toward the west and southwest, threatening to encircle the 3rd Division's positions. Again the II Corps commander requested permission to pull all his forces back to the immediate edge of Viipuri but was allowed to withdraw only the 3rd Division as far as Patterinmaki in the middle of the city. When the retreat got underway, the Russians followed close behind. However, the Finnish units were able to set the southern outskirts on fire that night to slow the enemy down.

Later that night, the 5th Division managed to get the situation at Tammisuo under control, isolating the enemy tanks from their infantry. This success conducted by the 1st Battalion of the 15th Infantry improved the situation somewhat for the time being.

While the 3rd and 5th Divisions had been fighting in front of Viipuri, the 23rd Division on their left (east) held the line from Tammisuo to Tali. From 8 March, the Russians hammered at the Finnish positions heavily until the very last minute of the war and were able to push the defenders some 10 kilometers further to the Karstilanjarvi-Leitimojarvi lakes support line.

During the 23rd Division's campaign on the Tali Line, engineers flooded the area for several kilometers around. This delayed the Russian advance, but it did not stop it. T-28 and T-35 tanks towed the lighter T-26s through water which was more than a meter deep in spots. In some cases Russian infantry waded up to their waists in sub-zero temperatures to continue the attack.

The Battle of the Viipuri Bay.

While II Corps held the Russian 7th Army at bay before Viipuri, one of the fiercest struggles of the Winter War developed on the ice and islands in the Gulf of Finland at Viipuri Bay. In order to deal with the situation effectively, Marshal Mannerheim placed the forces defending the Gulf and Bay under a new command on 1 March. The new organization, called the Coast Group, was placed under the leadership of the Chief of the General Staff, Lieutenant General L. Oesch. His troops consisted of the 4th Division and a number of battalions and batteries including those which had been transferred from the Lapland Front in late February.

The winter of 1939-40 was one of the coldest on record, but until February the weather had been the invaluable ally of the hard pressed Finns. Now, when spring should have helped them by breaking up the ice, winter held on to the advantage of the Russians. By this time, the ice was strong enough to carry the weight of tanks, and the lanes cut in the ice by engineers froze over almost immediately. When the retreat of the Finnish forces to the rear positions was completed, two islands, Tuppura and Uuras, were still occupied by the Finns, although they were outside of the Tali Line. These islands guarding the mouth of Viipuri Bay had been essential for the protection of the retreating forces. Once the rear positions were reached, the Finnish forces found themselves with an additional 30 kilometers to defend because of the thick ice on the bay. Therefore, the islands continued to be important because the Russians had massed four divisions and a number of armored units southwest of Uuras.

Tuppura Island was attacked on 2 March and was lost after several assaults had been repulsed. After the first few failures, the 7th Army had developed a successful tactic for taking an island. They bombarded it by artillery and air and then surrounded it with tanks, thus cutting off the defenders from the mainland. The tanks then tightened the cordon and kept the defenders under mortar and small arms fire, after which the infantry made the final assault. This tactic was used throughout the island hopping operation. In most cases, the Finnish troops were able to break through the perimeter of tanks and to retreat to the mainland.

The loss of Tuppura and Uuras was a severe blow to the Finns; however, Teikari Island in Russian hands was a matter of greater importance. It stands in front of Vilaniemi Cape on the north shore of the bay, but also protected the forces holding Suonio Island, a key in the defense system of the bay. Two attempts to capture the island on 2 March failed; however, it was finally lost and the Russians used it as a base for their landing on the north shore of Viipuri Bay at Vilaniemi and Haranpaanniemi Capes.

A Finnish counterattack during the night of 2-3 March managed to push the enemy forces back on the ice, but the following day, the Russians captured their previous foothold. Once again, the Russian force, consisting of three divisions, was beaten back with the aid of some reinforcements. The mainland was again in Finnish hands.

By 4 March, the outer islands were abandoned in the face of the overwhelming enemy forces. Several counterattacks during the previous days had thinned the ranks of the defenders to such an extent that they had to be sent to the rear for rest and recuperation.

A general attack against all the Finnish positions commenced on 4 March. The enemy formations even came across the ice of the Gulf of Finland on this occasion, advancing from their bases on the islands of Suursaari, Lavansaari and Someri, which are in the middle of the Gulf, toward the cities of Kotka and Hamina, far west from Viipuri. These advances, however, were checked by the Finnish coast artillery batteries located along the southern coast of Finland. The advancing Russian forces were beaten back by the exploding shells which broke up the ice, drowning large numbers of the attackers and causing panic among the survivors. These advances caused the Finnish high command to strengthen the coastal defences further to the west. A battalion of young boys and men too old for military service was assembled in a hurry and sent to the coast as reinforcements.

The cause of the greatest concern was the magnitude of the attacking force on Viipuri Bay, which endangered the defenses of Viipuri. The Russians directed their heaviest artillery and air bombardment at Vilaniemi Cape, and launched an infantry regiment and a battalion of tanks against the defenders. They soon had a foothold in the village, with an estimated two divisions coming in behind them by nightfall. The situation within Haranpaaniemi Cape-Vilajoki Village, Vilaniemi Cape-Heinlahti Bay was serious. During the night, however, the 9th Infantry Regiment, the only reserve the Finnish II Corps commander had, was sent to reinforce the defenders.

Meanwhile, farther down the bay towards Viipuri, another Russian attack group was ready to assault Suonio Island from Uuras Island which had just been evacuated. Enemy attacks at other points in the bay had been repulsed. Until that date, the Coast group had held its own, but it could not hope to do so any longer without more help. All the reserves had been committed, and the artillery batteries were in desperate need of ammunition. The II Corps had 600 artillery rounds in the stockpile, which had to satisfy the needs of three divisions and the Coast group, all of which were under constant attack.

By the morning of 5 March, the 7th Army was firmly on the north shore of Viipuri Bay. During that day, the Russians assaulted all the island positions, to include those immediately in front of Viipuri. The lanes in the ice made by the engineers immediately froze solid, and the Russian tanks drove across them at will.

By this time, the 7th Army was attacking the Viipuri Bay with three of the four divisions there, and 16 divisions were operating against the whole Viipuri Front from the Bay to the Vuoksi River, while another ten divisions operated from there to Lake Ladoga. The Finnish Army had the Coast group and six less than half strength divisions on the Viipuri Front with no reserves, and ammunition stocks dangerously low. On the other hand, the Red Army had an unlimited source of supplies and men. Furthermore, the roads on the Finnish side were choked with refugees and supply traffic. The problem of movement of supplies was compounded by constant air attacks. As soon as the Russians gained a foothold on the north shore of the Bay, the Finnish supply situation became almost impossible. In spite of these difficulties, the Finns had no choice but to fight on. The Russians had the initiative and they used it to the fullest advantage. On 6 March, Russian troops occupied part of the Nisolahti Village, while another group penetrated the Finnish line at Niskapohja. By mid day, they had established a beachhead on Turkinsaari Island and Majapohja.

By nightfall on 6 March, the situation was so desperate that the commander of the 4th Division considered withdrawing his east flank back so far that it would have exposed the right flank of the 3rd Division which was without reserves; its 9th regiment had already been employed on the Coast group sector. The 4th Division commander also requested reinforcements to hold Neulasaari Island where he feared a major breakthrough. But all that could be spared was an understrength company from the 5th Division far away to the north of Viipuri.

It was only a question of time before the whole island defense system crumbled and the Finns would be forced to withdraw to the north shore. When this happened, the entire west flank of the II Corps and the supply lines running northwest around Viipuri would become untenable.

Throughout 7 March, the 7th Army pushed forward, while its artillery and supporting air force pounded the Finnish positions and supply lines. The Viipuri-Hamina road was cut at Vilaniemi Cape, making it necessary to bypass that area. By the same evening, it was evident that the island defenses from Suonionsaari Island to Majapohja were untenable. Their defenders were withdrawn the next day after savage battles.

One by one, the islands had been abandoned, and the Finns were fighting primarily on the mainland, except for Piispansaari Island where a small unit was still holding out. Between Vilajoki and Nisalahti villages, no changes of any significance had occurred, in spite of fierce battles.

An even more massive attack began on 9 March. Finnish reconnaissance reported that a ten kilometer long column of Russian troops and tanks was crossing the ice between Pullinniemi Cape and Maisalansaari Island and Vilaniemi Cape, where it was estimated that two divisions were already in action. At the same time, the commander of the Finnish 4th Division was worried about his troops on Piispansaari Island. That evening, the island was abandoned. This move allowed the Russians to penetrate the line between the forces of the Coast group and the II Corps. The 14th Infantry Regiment, reinforced by a weak battalion from the 3rd Division, had to be sent in to seal the gap before the rear positions were completely enveloped.

On 10 March, the Russians attempted to roll up the Finnish defenses at Majapohja

and simultaneously attacked Porkansaari Island, the only island still remaining in Finnish hands. In spite of their exhaustion, the troops of the 4th Division made a counterattack which was at first successful but was finally repulsed. By that night, the Russians were in possession of both Majapohja and Porkansaari Island.

While the battle was raging further up the bay at Vilaniemi, the Russians were using their fresh troops for further advance. Wherever they created a dent in the line, they quickly pushed beyond the Viipuri-Hamina road, thus gaining a deepened and extended front. But even with new troops and their better positions, however, the Red Army was unable to make a breakthrough.

The situation was verging on disaster for the Finnish Army, should any one point give way completely. Regardless of their condition, Finnish troops held out and the Russian drive to reach Viipuri from the north shore was halted.

On 11 March, the enemy again made a push but was stoutly resisted. Again on the 12th, they tried to break through the line between the 4th Division and II Corps, causing the defenders to pull back up to Ahokas-Vainikki area on the mainland. On the 12th, the Russians continued to attack up to the moment when the ceasefire went into effect. Apparently they hoped to break through and move on to capture Viipuri, their ultimate goal.

Even though the ceasefire was agreed to begin at 1100 hours, 13 March, the Red Army continued action for an hour more. For example, a Russian battalion continued to attack the 15th Infantry Regiment sector at Rotanpesa, south of Tammisuo. Forty Finnish soldiers who obeyed the order and did not resist were taken prisoners. They were, however, released on the following day. On the East Karelian front, a Finnish platoon was surrounded by the Russians; they, too, were taken prisoners but were never repatriated.

CHAPTER IV - Reflections: The Agony of the War

The Status of Finnish Forces During the Last Days of the War.

The crux of the peril was the manpower shortage. With progressively thinning forces, the strength of battalions being below 250, the question was how much longer the inevitable collapse could be delayed. Even the quality of the last available replacements was much below standards. Men in their mid 50s and high school boys, hastily trained, and recuperating returnees from hosptials could not be expected to perform miracles.

Perhaps an even more crucial problem was the lack of artillery, especially ammunition (when the battle of Viipuri began, II Corps had less than a thousand rounds of artillery ammunition). Most of the artillery was pre-World War I stock consisting of numerous models and calibers which caused almost unsurmountable logistical problems. The resourcefulness of the Finnish commanders was severely tested in utilizing their very limited resources. Frequently an infantry battalion was the largest reserve available to a division commander while simultaneous attacks were being conducted at various points along his entire front of responsibility. Reserves shuttled frequently from one trouble spot to another, under constant danger from the air while enroute to the next battle area. The attacking forces succeeded in penetrating the front lines at numerous points. Most of the attacks, however, were repulsed, often only by counterattacks at night; and every such action took its toll in lives. There were companies and even battalions which lost their commanders three times a day. There were companies which had lost all their officers by the end of

January. Several officers had to be released because of a fatigue or loss of nerves.

Damage to the defense works was serious. Trenches, dugouts (korsus), automatic weapons' positions and other field installations were pulverized by artillery barrages. Sometimes a single artillery round or an aerial bomb on a shelter killed an entire squad or even a larger group.

The Last Evaluation of the Situation

On 9 March, Marshal Mannerheim requested the Isthmus Army commander, General Heinrichs to prepare an evaluation of the situation concerning the status of his forces, their remaining capabilities and limitations. The following are excerpts of his report:

> As commander of the Isthmus Army, I consider it my duty to report that the present state of the army is such that continued operations can lead to nothing but further debilitation and new losses of territory. In support of my view, I set forth the loss of personnel which has occurred and which is still going on. The battle strength of battalions is reported now generally to be below 250 men, with the aggregate daily casualties rising into the thousands.
>
> As a consequence of physical and spiritual exhaustion, the battle fitness of those who remain is not what it was when the war started. Considerable losses of officers further reduce the utility of these diminished units. Through enemy artillery fire, our machine gun and anti-tank weapons have been demolished to such an extent that a noticeable lack is generally

> apparent on critical fronts. Since, in addition, events on the right flank have made indispensable fresh expenditures of troops on unprepared terrain and at the expense of the present front, the endurance of our defense has been critically weakened. Enemy air activity frequently makes the transfer and maintenance of forces decidedly difficult. The commander of the Coast group, Lieutenant General Oesch, has emphasized to me the scanty numbers and the moral exhaustion of his forces, and does not seem to believe he can succeed with them. The commander of the II Army Corps, Lieutenant General Ohquist, has expressed the opinion that if no surprises take place, his present front may last a week, but no longer, depending upon how the personnel, especially the officer corps, is used. The commander of the III Corps, Major General Talvela, expressed his view by saying that everything is hanging by a thread.

At the time of the above report, Marshal Mannerheim, together with the Finnish government, had to weigh the possibility that an Anglo-French expeditionary force would come to Finland's rescue, but without the guaranteed success.

From 8 February to 7 March, the expeditionary forces' timetables and probable strengths varied considerably. The last information reaching Finland indicated that 57,000 French, British and Polish troops would be sent, and that the first echelon of 15,500 men could be in Finland by the end of March.

As the above situation report indicates, Marshal Mannerheim had to recommend to the Finnish government that a ceasefire must be negotiated and concluded before the front collapsed. His view was also decisive. President Kallio admitted to a change of mind when he heard the report on the military situation. After midnight, 9 March 1940, it was finally decided, with two Cabinet ministers still opposed, to authorize the delegation in Moscow to use their own discretion about the terms of peace, provided it was an unanimous agreement.

The final moments were at hand. The Allies continued to press the Finns to request their aid. However, in spite of the new Soviet demands which seemed to be aimed at Sweden, the transit rights for the Allies were refused by the Swedish government. At that time, neither Marshal Mannerheim nor Vaino Tanner, the Foreign Minister of Finland, considered the proposed Allied expedition militarily significant.

Early in the morning of 11 March, he Finnish Cabinet concurred with Foreign Minister Tanner's proposal that the Soviet terms be accepted, and shortly thereafter the Foreign Relations Committee of the Parliament voted 13-4 in favor of that course. Within four hours, that was known to a Swedish news bureau in Stockholm and, in spite of Minister Tanner's efforts to prevent it, it appeared in the afternoon papers. This was Sweden's final serious disservice to Finland during the war. The Russian negotiators used these reports to their advantage at that day's bargaining session.

The Peace Treaty of Moscow

On 12 March, Russian Foreign Minister Molotov presented his final draft of the treaty to the Finnish delegation, and the delegation requested from Helsinki full powers to sign. The Finnish Cabinet met in the morning to face the final bitter decision. At that late hour, the lure of the Allied expedition still concerned them. Troop ships were actually loading in British harbors and, late in the evening, both Chamberlain and Daladier publicly announced their readiness to send assistance, if the Finnish government requested it. The majority of the Cabinet supported Foreign Minister Tanner's recommendation that the treaty be signed at once.

President Kallio reluctantly agreed to sign the credentials to be sent to Moscow. On signing them, the elderly president paraphrased an Old Testament verse, saying: "May the hand wither which is forced to sign such a paper." Five months later his right arm was paralyzed by a stroke, and within the year he was dead.

At 1600 hours, 12 March 1940, Radio Moscow announced the signing of the peace treaty, but no official word was received on that day. In the evening the British Minister called on Minister Tanner to advise him, in a confidence not to be disclosed to the Norwegian or Swedish governments, that the expedition would be sent without their consent, if the Finns would publicly request it.

At 0230 hours, 13 March, Minister Tanner received from Stockholm the text of the protocol to the treaty which defined the provisions for the ceasefire and troop withdrawals. Finally, at 0600 hours, a cable from Moscow arrived confirming that the treaty had become effective on the previous evening. The long ordeal of agonizing indecision was over, and the race against total disaster had been won.

The Results of the War for Finland

For Finland, the Winter War held even greater significance than for the Russians. The nation's human losses were 23,157 killed in action, and 43,557 others were wounded. In terms of combat statistics, the old proverb, "One Finn is always worth ten Russians," was almost exactly true. In proportion to the national populations of Russia and Finland, however, Finnish losses were much more tragic than those of the Soviet Union.

For Finns, the ultimate meaning of the costly war was the fact that the peace was not signed between the Kuusinen's puppet "government" (People's Democratic Republic of Finland) and Stalin but between the real government of Finland and the Soviet Union. The Finns had retained that which they had waited so long to achieve, their freedom and independence. The entire nation had also experienced a heartening sense of unity completely unprecedented in the short history of the Republic. Marshal Mannerheim summarized the meaning of this so concisely and eloquently:

> May coming generations not forget the dearly bought lessons of our defensive war. They can with pride look back on the Winter War and find courage and confidence in its glorious history. That an Army so inferior in numbers and equipment should have inflicted such serious defeats on an overwhelmingly powerful enemy, and while retreating, have over and over again repelled his attacks, is something for which it is hard to find a parallel in the history of war. But it is equally admirable that the Finnish people, face to face with an apparently hopeless situation, were able to resist a feeling of despair and, instead, to grow in devotion and greatness. Such a nation has earned the right to live.

The Results of the War for the Soviet Union

Precise Soviet casualties during the war may never be known, but they were unquestionably enormous. The truth lies somewhere between Molotov's admission of 48,745 killed in action and 158,863 wounded and the figure of one million two hundred thousand given by Khrushchev. The most reliable Finnish source estimated Russian losses at 175,000-200,000 killed in action and two to three hundred thousand wounded, to include those who became unfit for combat due to cold injuries. The Soviet official history merely acknowledges that their casualties were "excessive and avoidable."

Another negative result was the loss of prestige of the Soviet armed forces. The fiascoes of the early phase, such as Suomussalmi-Raate-Kuhmo campaigns, and the later Russian defeats on the Ladogan-Karelian front, received more worldwide attention than the successes of the later stages on the Karelian Isthmus. A semi-professional British magazine, thc Fighting Forces, proclaimed that "the vaunted worth of the Russian Army has proved to be a myth." "A giant with feet of clay" was the expression of another critic.

Contrary to a popular misconception, however, Hitler did not miscalculate Soviet strength because of the winter War. In a letter to Mussolini on 8 March 1940, he noted:

> ".... The criticisms which have been made of the Russian soldiers in consequence of the operations to date are not borne out by reality and the facts. Taking into consideration the available supply facilities, no power in the world would have been able, except after the most thoroughgoing preparations, to achieve any other results at 30 to 40 degrees below

> zero (C) on such terrain than did the Russians at the very first."

Marshal Mannerheim was probably correct in considering the loss of prestige of the Soviet armed forces the most significant international result of the war. There were several military lessons which the Soviet army learned in its "acid test" as General Zhukov termed the war. A special session of the Main Military Council was convened in the Kremlin in 14-17 April 1940, to analyze the "wrongs" noted during the war. Among other things, the speakers criticized the following:

a. The unwieldy organization of the infantry division.

b. The low level of combat proficiency of the individual infantrymen.

c. The inadequacy of infantry firepower.

d. The lack of winter clothing and over snow mobility equipment.

e. The lack of cold weather training.

f. The shortcomings in troop supply and maintenance of equipment.

The council passed a resolution entitled "Measures to be taken in combat training, organization, and structure of the troops of the Red Army on the basis of the experience of the war in Finland and the combat experience of recent years."

One of the most important changes in the command structure came about in an order by the Presidium of the Supreme Soviet of the USSR on 12 August 1940, which reinstated the unitary command system in the Soviet armed forces. This reform downgraded the political commissar from a status of co-equal with the military commander to that of a deputy commander for political affairs. As a result of the many reforms, ranks of generals, marshals and admirals were reinstituted in May 1940.

The Red Army organization became more rational. The Russian forces the Finns encountered in the Continuation War in 1941 were organized into light or heavy battalions, regiments and divisions depending on the terrain and the mission. The most prominent change within the Soviet forces, however, was their winter warfare capability.
Timoshenko, who became a Marshal of the Soviet Union and succeeded Viroshilov as Defense Commissar in the spring of 1940, mentioned to a military attache in Moscow, "the Russians have learned much in this hard war in which the Finns fought with heroism."

The Russian Viewpoint of the Winter War as Seen by Mr. Khrushchev

Mr. Khrushchev, one of Stalin's trustees since the Russian revolution and later a dictator himself, gives his version of the Winter War in his memoirs, "Khrushchev Remembers:"

> Whenever I came to Moscow from Kiev, Stalin almost always summoned me. Occasionally I found him alone when I went to see him. It was always easier to exchange opinions with him candidly if we were alone. But much more often than not, Stalin had Molotov, Voroshilov, Kaganovich, and sometimes Zhdanov with him when I called on him. Zhdanov was the first Secretary of the Leningrad Regional Committee. Mikoyan and Beria were often there, too. One day when I came to Moscow, Stalin invited me to his apartment for dinner. He told me Molotov and Kuusinen would be there.

Kuusinen was then attached to the Comintern. When I arrived at Stalin's apartment in the Kremlin, I had the feeling that Stalin, Molotov, and Kuusinen were continuing an earlier conversation about Finland. Apparently they had already decided to present Finland with an ultimatum.

It had been agreed that Kuusinen would head the government of a new Karelo-Finnish Soviet Socialist Republic (SSR). Up to that time, Karelia had been an autonomous republic annexed to the Russian Federation. Now Karelia was to be made a Union Republic. The consensus of the group was that the Finns should be given one last chance to accept the territorial demands which they had already rejected during the unsuccessful negotiations. If they didn't yield to our ultimatum, we would take military action. This was Stalin's idea. Naturally I didn't oppose him. Besides, in this case I agreed that it was the right thing to do. All we had to do was raise our voice a little bit, and the Finns would obey. If that didn't work, we would fire one shot and the Finns would put up their hands and surrender. Or so we thought. When I arrived at the apartment, Stalin was saying, "Let's get started today."

We sat around for a long time. The hour of the ultimatum had already been set. After the prescribed time had elapsed, Artillery Marshal Kulic was dispatched to supervise the bombardment of the Finnish border. We waited to see what would happen. Stalin was confident. None of us thought there would be a war. We were sure that the Finns would accept our demands without forcing us to go to war.

Suddenly there was a telephone call. We had fired our salvo, and the Finns had replied with artillery fire of their own. De facto, the war had begun. There is, of course, another version of the facts: It is said that the Finns started shooting first and that we were compelled to shoot back. It is always like that when people start a war. They say, "You fired the first shot," or "You slapped me first, and I'm only hitting back." There is some question about whether we had any legal or moral right for our actions against Finland. Of course we didn't have any legal right. As far as morality is concerned, our desire to protect ourselves was ample justification in our own eyes.

A few days after the war began, I left for Ukraine. Like everyone else, I was confident that our advantage would prove immeasurable and that our dispute with the Finns would be solved quickly, without many casualties for us. So we thought, so we hoped. But the history of that conflict turned out very differently. The war dragged on stubbornly. The Finns turned out to be good warriors. They had organized

their defenses brilliantly along the Mannerheim Line on the Karelian Isthmus, and they thwarted our attempt to push through this strategically important passage.
We soon realized we had bitten off more than we could chew, our casualties mounted alarmingly. In the winter it was decided to bypass the Karelian Isthmus and to strike a blow from Lake Ladoga to the north where there are no fortifications. But when we tried to strike from the rear, we found ourselves in an even more difficult situation than before. Our army encountered very mobile ski troops armed with automatic high velocity rifles. We tried to put our own troops on skiis, too, but it wasn't easy for ordinary, untrained Red Army soldiers to fight on skiis. We started intensively to recruit professional sportsmen. There weren't many around. We had to bring them from Moscow and Ukraine as well as from Leningrad, poor fellows, they were ripped to shreds. I don't know how many came back alive. This was terrible time, terrible because of our losses, and even more terrible in the wider perspective. The Germans were watching with undisguised glee as we took a drubbing from the Finns.
Our navy was engaged against the Finnish fleet. You wouldn't have thought that the Finns would have the advantage at sea, but our navy couldn't

do anything right. I remember hearing when I was at Stalin's in Moscow that one of our submarines had been unable to sink a Swedish merchant vessel which it had mistaken for a Finnish ship. The Germans observed this incident and gave us a teasing pinch by offering their assistance.

I recall how Stalin spoke with bitterness and sadness about the way the war was going, Stalin was furious with the military and with Voroshilov, Commissar of Defense for many years. Voroshilov deserved to bear the brunt of the blame for the way the Finnish war was going, but he wasn't the only guilty party. He blamed the mishandling of the war on faulty inteligence.

I remember once at the nearby Dacha, Stalin Jumped up in a white hot rage and started to berate Voroshilov. Voroshilov was also boiling mad. He leaped up, turned red, and hurled Stalin's accusations back into his face. "You have yourself to blame for all this!" shouted Voroshilov. "You are the one who annihilated the Old Guard of the army; you had our best generals killed!" Stalin rebuffed him, and at that, Voroshilov picked up a platter with a roast suckling pig on it and smashed it on the table. Voroshilov ended up being relieved of his duties as People's Commissar of Defense. Marshal Timoshenko, who was commander of the Kiev Military District, came to me in Kiev and said, "I have been summoned to Moscow. I will almost certainly be going to the Finnish Front." He was put in charge of our troops on the Karelian Isthmus, replacing Meretskov.

Our army had learned its lesson. It was decided not to circle around and strike from the rear but to hit frontally, to crush the Finnish fortifications on the Karelian Isthmus. The necessary artillery, air power, and infantry were concentrated for the strike. The Finnish pillboxes were wiped out. Nothing was left standing in front of our artillery. The air force played its part in the strike, too. I remember Stalin saying, very typically, "Our air force has been called into action. The assignment is to demolish the Finnish supply lines to the front, knock the railroads out of commission, bomb the bridges, and strafe the locomotives. Many bridges have been destroyed. Many trains have been crippled. The Finns have only their skiis left. Finns can never be without their skiis. Their supply of skiis never runs out."

Finland called for a truce. Negotiations began. We agreed on the terms for peace and signed a treaty. And so the war with Finland ended. We started to analyze the reasons why we were so badly prepared and why the war had cost us so dearly. I would say we lost as many as a million lives. Timoshenko told me that faulty intelligence had not been to blame after all. In fact, it was learned that our intelligence service had known about the Finnish defenses all along. The pillboxes and artillery batteries of the Mannerheim Line had even been drawn on our intelligence maps before the war. The trouble was that no intelligence officers had been consulted when our first strike was planned. I cannot imagine how this kind of stupidity was permitted. If we had only deployed our forces against the Finns in the way even a child could have figured by looking at a map, things would have turned out differently for both the Soviet Union and Finland. The Winter War with Finland showed us our very serious weaknesses. It also exposed our weaknesses to Hitler. It does not take much imagination to guess what Hitler must have concluded after he watched us try to wage war against the Finns: "The Soviet Union has barely managed to handle a country that we could have disposed of in a few hours. What would be left of the Russians if we attacked them with our best equipment and masses of our best trained, best organized troops?" In short, our miserable conduct of the Finnish campaign encouraged Hitler in his plans for the blitzkrieg, his Operation Barbarossa.

In our war against the Finns we had an opportunity to choose the time and place. We outnumbered the enemy, and we had all the time in the world to prepare for our operation. Yet even in the most favorable conditions it was only after great difficulty and enormous losses that we were finally able to win. A victory at such a cost was actually a moral defeat. Our people never knew that we had suffered a moral defeat, of course, because they were never told the truth. Quite the contrary. When the Finnish war ended, our country was told, "Let the trumpets of victory sound!" But the seeds of doubt had been sown. The war against the Finns was a dark hour for our army, whose slogan of invincibility was, "In case there's a war tomorrow, we are ready for the march today!"

CHAPTER V - Lessons Learned

The Setting is the Enemy

The peculiarities of the Finnish theater of war that caused the greatest combat difficulties were the absolute lack of roads and the close character of the terrain which, with its vest zone of virgin forests, is so very different from the European landscape in latitudes farther south. The Karelian woods are under no forestry management such as is commonly applied in central Europe. The primeval forest is the result of natural reseeding. Old and young stands of trees are intermingled and frequently give rise to impenetrable thickets. This boundless forest is virtually unexplored. Throughout the trackless, desolate region, deepest solitude and deathly silence reign supreme. Lakes, swamps, moors, and loose rock are characteristic of the Karelian landscape. Although on the Karelian Isthmus (the corridor between the Gulf of Finland and Lake Lagoda) and in the area between Lake Lagoda and Lake Onega the woods in some places are very dense and include old stands of trees, the timber becomes lighter and weaker the farther one goes north, until at last only scattered trees and bushes extend upward from an inextricable tangle of large rocks. In the Far North, rocky ground covered with reindeer moss, lichens, and blueberry, cranberry, and juniper bushes predominates in the wilderness. In the part of Karelia between Lake Onega and the White Sea, the tree line is about five hundred feet above sea level. Birches grow on the slopes between the conifer covered dales and the bare tops of the mountains, which are less than a thousand feet high. The conifers disappear completely north of the Arctic Circle. This is a favorable region for birch forests, so characteristic of Lapland, with their short trunks often branching out like bushes. In the Petsamo region the

completely treeless tundra extends up to the coast, where it changes into bare shingle along the Arctic Ocean.
This is a heroic landscape which has remained completely untouched by modern civilization. Since the dim past little or nothing has changed there. As in those days of long ago described in the songs of the Finnish epic, the "Kalevala," the hunter and fisher, the Lapp nomad with his reindeer herds, the individual loving solitude lives in the primeval wilderness, constantly struggling with the forces of nature.

The Operational Mobility of Army Corps and Divisions

Before World War II the Finns estimated that they could adequately defend their country. The more than 1,200 kilometers southeastern and eastern border of Finland which was primarily considered to be the future theater of war, had a very sparse network of roads, which would restrict the utilization of strong forces. It was estimated that the enemy could concentrate at most 15 divisions as compared to Finland's 10 divisions.
From the approximately 100 kilometers wide Karelian Isthmus, four railroads and 3 to 10 highways led to the northwest. The railroads were single tracked; the roads had a gravel surface and were so narrow that a two way truck traffic was barely possible. The surface of the roads was estimated to be so poor, that only one infantry division with reinforcements could advance along the direction of one road.
In the part of Karelia just north of Lake Ladoga, an area 100 kilometers wide, one railroad and four highways led from east to west. The border from Lake Ladoga to the Arctic Ocean was approximately 1,100 kilometers long. A total of six roads ran from here to east and west. These roads were in a much poorer condition than those on the Karelian Isthmus. Along these roads as well, the advance

of only one division was regarded as possible. Since nearly 80 percent of the frontier region was covered by forests and 15 percent by marsh lands, the 200 kilometers wide sectors between the roads were uninhabited areas of forests, marshes and lakes. Seldom were the winters so intensely cold, that the ice on the marsh lands and the lakes would be strong enough to bear the weight of tanks, heavy guns and trucks.

At first, during the winter of 1939-1940, there was very little snow, but the temperature fell to -40°C. Nowhere was the snow cover as deep as one meter. The surface of the bad roads, the marsh lands and the lakes were so solidly frozen that they supported the weight of even heavy transport vehicles. The development of snowplowing equipment and of motor vehicles adequate for winter conditions made it possible for the enemy to use nearly 50 divisions in the final stages of the war. The situation became extremely critical on the coast of the Gulf of Finland, between Viipuri and Hamina, where seven divisions attacked across the ice of Viipuri Bay. However, the greatest surprise was that between Lake Ladoga and the Arctic Ocean, 11 divisions operated from the beginning of the war and 20 in the end. The enemy's complete command of the air, 1,000 aircraft in comparison to 100, made possible the movements of dense and direct concentrations even on the ice flats.

The Finnish army corps and divisions did not derive much advantage from the increased freedom of operations, because they had very few motor vehicles and the existing road network was thus sufficient for their operations. On the other hand, the Finns had improved the armament, equipment and tactics of the infantry and continued to do so by improvisation. Primarily, the aim of these innovations was to use the forests and the climate to the best possible advantage. The key problems to solve were, first, how to survive in the severe winter weather in the uninhabited wilderness, and, second, how to operate in the deep forests flanking the roads.

Weather and Terrain Effects Upon Operations

Experiences gained during the Finnish-Soviet Winter War of 1939-40 had taught the following lessons:

First, the natural conditions along the frontier between Finland and the Soviet Union, the extremely extensive, pathless wasteland of the frontier region, the uneven terrain covered with loose rock and consequently passable only with difficulty, and the negligible development of roads are not suited to operations with large masses of troops of low mobility. Over broad stretches of country it is, in many cases, impossible to conduct operations involving large organizations, and in some instances, it is pointless.

Second, from the strategic point of view, the importance of the different sectors of the frontier region varies widely. Gain or loss of areas far removed from any kind of communication is of no decisive importance to the further course of the war.

Third, the characteristics of terrain and climate in the Far North are such that winter is the more favorable season for offensive campaigns, while summer is more suitable for defensive operations. Early and late winter are particularly favorable for attack operations; mid-winter with its deep snow is a less appropriate time for offensive warfare.

Fourth, the transitions from winter to summer and from summer to winter constitute the muddy periods when use of the roads temporarily ceases or is greatly limited. The muddy period in the fall does not last as long as that in the spring. Because of the hard granite soil of Finland and Russian Karelia, the roads usually dry out much quicker there than in southern Russia. In the Far North, the principal concern is the melting of the snow which has fallen during the winter. The Finns have great experience and have developed special techniques to keep the main highways free from snow and open throughout the winter for the use of mail trucks and buses. The effect of brief periods of rain, which in Russia proper turn the roads into a hopeless condition, is negligible in Finland and the border area. During the muddy season, especially in the spring, there is no chance for effective air support because it is impossible for units of any considerable size to take off from the completely flooded airfields. Provisions were made to maintain flying operations on a limited scale through installation of latticed wooden runways. In these cases, it was necessary to park the airplanes either on the runways or in their immediate vicinity. Such a procedure cannot be applied for organizations of any considerable size unless one accepts the necessity of expending enormous amounts of material and labor in the construction of latticed wooden runways and taxiing strips to the hardstands. Sincc both opponents were faced by identical conditions, air force activity, with only a few exceptions, was almost completely suspended on both sides during the muddy season.

The Horse Provides Tactical Mobility

Finnish farmers and lumberjacks were used to transportation with horses and sleighs in winter conditions. When hauling logs from the forests to the roads, the preliminary stage was to move on skis and open a trail in the woods, avoiding gorges, cliffs and steep rises. This was not too difficult, because the differences of level in the Finnish terrain are only about ten meters. When a few horses and a sleigh had moved along the trail, the worst ruggednesses could be noticed and avoided. A winter road was finally formed in the forest, along which a horse could pull a load weighing up to one ton.

In the pre-war winter maneuvers of the army, the methods of the farmers and the lumberjacks had been used. Sleighs, sleds and skis were chosen and developed in such a way that they could transport the heavy arms and equipment of the infantry in the roadless forests and across the frozen marshes. Light horse drawn artillery was loaded on sleighs or runners were fixed to wheels. Sleighs were much better for evacuating the wounded than vehicles on wheels in the summer. Transferring the traffic from roads to forests, in shelter from observation and air reconnaissance, offered new possibilities for surprising the adversary and reducing the advantage of his air superiority.

In 1939, there were about 500,000 horses in the country, but during mobilization the armed forces used only 20 percent of them. Because more than a half of the nearly 500,000 army reservists called up were farmers or lumberjacks, the number of skilled horsemen was equivalent to that of horses. Considering the fact that all the Finnish soldiers were used to winter conditions and to moving in the dense forests, the tactical mobility of the army was on a very high level. The capability of imaginative innovations and successful improvisations contributed to this tactical efficiency.

Effects of Snow, Ice and Frost on Operations and Firepower

The effect of snow, ice and frost on firepower could not be estimated beforehand. Not until after the experiences of the summer of 1941 and the battles of 1944 could the weakening impact of snow and frost on firepower be adequately observed. It has not been possible to measure exactly this impact, but those who have seen service in the wars of 1939-1945 calculate that snow and subarctic weather lessened firepower by at least one third or even by 50 percent.

First, deep snow reduces fragmentation in the same way as soft soil does. Frost affects primers, so that the number of dud shells grows considerably. The power of an exploding shell is somewhat smaller in subarctic weather, and the accuracy of fire weaker because the powder burns more slowly. Cold weather also increases the mistakes of an observer directing artillery fire. Frost does not have a direct effect on the firepower of the light arms of the infantry, but accuracy of fire suffers due to the human factor; that is, the effect of sub-zero weather on the soldier. Automatic weapons and machine guns are heavily affected by freezing weather.
According to the nearly unanimous opinion of men who saw service in all phases of the war, the enemy had much weaker firepower and worse accuracy of fire than the Finnish troops, accustomed to and prepared for winter conditions. There was an especially big difference in the power and accuracy of the light arms of the infantry. The Finns had to pay attention to the effects of winter and severe cold in the yearly winter contests, in which the army and the Civic Guard took part. In winter conditions, it was necessary to keep especially the automatic weapons very clean, to prevent freezing of the moving parts. Sometimes arms had to be cleaned with petroleum when no light sewing machine oil was available. This kind of oil would not freeze and had a viscosity rate which made it suitable for all types of automatic arms. Besides the freeze endurance of the usual lubricating oils, it was necessary to test and pay attention to the anti-freeze capacity of other fluids and oils as well to keep the weapons in action. For the handling of weapons, knitted gloves, with only the trigger finger free, were found most suitable, these had been used by hunters for decades.
Since the Finns were accustomed to the climate, they clothed sensibly when winter set in. They knew how to dress when the temperature dipped several degrees below

zero. The field uniform of the soldier was designed to make him endure snow and freezing weather. The white dresses of the soldiers, covering the uniforms, had been developed for winter warfare.
The most difficult problem (solved, however, already in the 1930's) was how to camp and find shelter in the bitter winter of the wilderness. A tent for the use of half a platoon, approximately 20 men, was designed; this could be folded into a small and easily handled bundle. A portable box stove was enough to keep the tent warm even if the temperature fell to -40°C. On the stove coffee and food could be easily prepared. The new tent made military operations possible even in uninhabited areas.

Finnish "Motti" Tactics

Because the Finns had insufficient forces and equipment for classical air, tank and artillery operations, the enemy had to be forced to attack under the worst possible conditions for them. The terrain and the road network favored the Finns. The enemy divisions (or division) advanced along the road in a giant column, strung out over 100 kilometers. The road was flanked by a 100-200 kilometer wide, uninhabited wilderness, covered by forests, with numerous lakes and marshes.

("SA-kuva" - "Finnish Armed Forces photograph" in Finnish.)

The battalions engaged in delaying actions aimed at bringing the enemy's forward group to a halt in every possible location. At the same time, where the terrain and conditions were favorable, the enemy column was broken up and isolated into small units. The breaking up of the column was done by strike forces that advanced from the cover of the flanking wilderness toward the road used by the enemy. Short distance slicing operations were performed by mobile ski units; ammunition, mines and explosives were either carried along or pulled in sleds. The wounded were also evacuated in sleds. In medium distance, 10-20 kilometers, road cutting operations, a winter road was prepared and ammunition, mines and explosives as well as the wounded were moved through the woods by horses and sleighs. In long distance operations, a road was plowed at night on the snow covered ice of the marshes and lakes, and the troops and equipment were transported to within a distance of 5-10 kilometers of the enemy positions.

At the end of the winter (or ice) road, an easily defensible logistics base was established. Often it also served as an advanced dressing station, headed by a medical doctor. The attack, with the objective of cutting the road, was done on skis, while the equipment was carried and pulled on sleds, generally in short distance operations and under fire from enemy infantry. Such a base might have included a mortar company or even a battery of field artillery, which, however, for the sake of secrecy, withheld their fire until the infantry reached its objective and the general assault commenced.

The blocking points on the road along which the enemy advanced were decided upon and marked on the map after careful planning and reconnaissance. Along the road, one or several small hills or outcroppings in the terrain, without any organized defense, were usually chosen as points to block the road. Another requirement was that if the enemy tried to move forward or retreat, the road could be easily cut and brought under fire. The most advantageous from this operational point of view were bridges and embankments which were difficult to bypass.

The assault upon the point, which had been chosen for the roadblock, was done in the most surprising manner, taking the best possible advantage of the terrain and darkness. After the initial reconnaissance, the commander of the strike force or the battalion advanced with the orientation and reconnaissance group within observing distance of the final objective. On the basis of the information gained, by observing and listening to the enemy and the traffic along the road, the commander ordered the attack to begin at the very moment when few enemy troops were in the target area. The battalions of a strike force or the companies of a battalion advanced directly to those points in the terrain, which they had to occupy. The sappers of the attack group destroyed the bridges and embankments at the blocking points and mined the areas the enemy had to cross when counterattacking. Often there was enough time to prepare an improvised fire plan and to dig in at least into the snow before the enemy counterattacked. Each minute that passed before the counterattack began was to the advantage of the attack group blocking the road. The fire plan of the artillery was usually prepared to cover the most dangerous direction, but fire was opened only when the enemy's full counterattack began.

If the troops succeeded in completely surprising the enemy, as was often the case, effective counterattacks commenced only after several hours. Daylight favored the force that held the roadblock. The enemy's fire was inaccurate, because the troops were well hidden in the terrain. The fact that the enemy formations were at a close distance, with Finnish forces between the isolated groups, made the use of heavy weapons difficult, while making it possible for the Finns to fully exploit the accuracy of their light arms. The more numerous the roadblocks, the longer it took for the enemy to launch

their counterattacks and the more surely were they repelled.
The turning point in repelling the counterattacks was the separation of the tanks from the infantry following them. It was consequently important, that the positions of the infantry which blocked the road were in such rugged terrain or in such a dense forest, that the tanks were not able to drive inside them. If the positions fulfilled these requirements, the enemy's infantry was either annihilated or driven back. Finally, those tanks which had passed through the minefields were destroyed by attacking them with gasoline bottles and TNT-charges. During the Winter War and partly even during the Continuation War, the number of anti-tank guns was so limited that they could be used only when the enemy launched an armored attack along an open road.
Since the enemy forces were not able to move away from and maneuver outside the roads and since the supplies dropped from the air were insufficient, the counterattacks were in the end hampered by the lack of ammunition and food. The effects of the Arctic temperatures and the lack of tents and stoves contributed to the annihilation of the enemy forces between Lake Ladoga and the Arctic Ocean. On the Karelian Isthmus the Finnish "motti" tactics could not be used because of the continuous front lines and the dense network of roads.

The Finnish Troops

During early and late winter, troops equipped with skis and akios can operate off the roads and bring along all that is really needed for existence and for combat; but they must leave behind everything that cannot be carried easily through primeval forest or rocky wilderness. The superior skill of the Finnish troops in covering long distances gave them high mobility and consequently a decided ascendency over troops of the Red Army in the Winter War.

The Soviet command recognized the great importance of using skis in fighting in the Far North. According to Finnish accounts, the Russians formed and trained special elite ski units in Siberia and concentrated them before World War II on the eastern border of Finland. These Soviet troops soon acquired great skill and during the war became almost as good as the Finnish ski units, whose marching speed is surprisingly great even in especially difficult terrain. Combat operations even in trackless regions, are executed much faster on skis in winter than on foot in summer. The open flanks of the Finnish-German sectors between Lake Onega and the Arctic Ocean could only be effectively protected by mobile Finnish ski patrol detachments. The fight against the Soviet partisans was carried on by the Finns with the passion of skilled and experienced hunters. It was most successful in winter when the encmy's tracks could be followed in the snow, and they could be brought to bay.

The strength of the Finnish soldier lies in individual combat. The Finns possess an infallible instinct for finding their way in the dense growth of the pathless wilds. They are accurate trail readers and move noiselessly in the woods. Nothing is heard or seen of Finnish troops whether resting or marching, even from the closest proximity. Terrain training is of a very high order. A special technique for movement through woods has been developed and practiced so that the troops advance quickly, in the right direction and without losing contact. A Finnish company moves in the primeval forest just as smoothly and unerringly as a German company in the open landscape of central Europe. All Finns are enthusiastic hunters and sports lovers and fighting wakens in them all their hunting instincts.

Organization

The Finnish infantry is equipped with skis in winter. Accustomed from earliest infancy to move on skis during over half of the year, the Finn accomplishes marvels in covering long distances. The use of the simple Finnish toe binding enables the soldier to put on and take off his skis quickly. The enemy is approached on skis in small, well separated groups echeloned in depth. The crouching skiers, camouflaged in snow shirts, rapidly approach the enemy in short bounds. Just before the final rush, they quickly kick off their skies. Often the men drag their skis along, or else a member of the group gathers all the skis and brings them forward.

The Finnish cavalry in general had the mission of mounted infantry. The guiding principle in its training stressed encirclement and attack deep in the enemy flank. It was able to carry out this task because the Finnish horse was used to traveling even over difficult wooded terrain covered with rocky debris. In the winter the cavalry troops are also equipped with skis.

Training and organization of the Finnish artillery was primarily designed for combat in woods and achieved a high level of efficiency during the last war, despite the fact that the armament was to some extent old fashioned and lacked uniformity. Since opportunities for observation were limited in the wilderness, each battery, as a rule, needed several observation posts. Therefore, every battery had at least two forward observers. By means of a signal communication net specially organized for this purpose, every forward observer was able to deliver fire with all batteries of the regiment. In the defense it was even possible to deliver fire with all medium and heavy mortars. The forward observers of the mortars in turn were able to do the same. The forward observers were connected with the firing positions by wire and radio. Great stress was laid on surprise fires.

Survey was well perfected and very rapid when the aiming circle was employed.
In tank combat the Finns lacked practical experience. Not until World War II did the Finns undertake to organize an armored division. The materiel consisted of captured Russian equipment, to which a few German tanks were added in the last year of the war. Training was based on German regulations. The Karelian Isthmus is especially favorable for armored operations. The Russians employed numerous tank units there in the Winter War and in the summer of 1944.
The technical and tactical aspects of Finnish signal communications were still in the first stages of development. The use of bare wire, occasioned by special conditions of combat in woods and the critical situation in the manufacture of field signal cable, was remarkable. For this purpose, a galvanized iron wire 2mm thick was strung overhead. In winter, if the situation was urgent, it was also possible to utilize the insulating property of completely dry snow by laying wire in the snow as a metallic circuit. Messenger dogs and carrier pigeons were not used in the Finnish army.

Printed in Great Britain
by Amazon

41171675R00068